# Contemporary Color Theory and Use

# Contemporary Color Theory and Use

By Steven Bleicher

**THOMSON**

**DELMAR LEARNING** ™

Australia   Canada   Mexico   Singapore   Spain   United Kingdom   United States

## THOMSON

™

## DELMAR LEARNING

**Contemporary Color Theory and Use**
Steven Bleicher

**Vice President, Technology and Trades SBU:**
Alar Elken

**Editorial Director:**
Sandy Clark

**Senior Acquisitions Editor:**
James Gish

**Development Editor:**
Jaimie Wetzel

**Editorial Assistant:**
Marissa Maiella

**Marketing Director:**
Dave Garza

**Channel Manager:**
William Lawrensen

**Marketing Coordinator:**
Mark Pierro

**Production Director:**
Mary Ellen Black

**Production Manager:**
Larry Main

**Production Editor:**
Thomas Stover

**Art/Design Coordinator:**
Rachel Baker

**Cover Design:**
Helaine Cohn and Steven Bleicher

**Cover Art:**
John Labadie, *Search Engine*, digital "tabula rasa" image, 2000

Library of Congress
Cataloging-in-Publication Data

Bleicher, Steven.
  Contemporary color theory & use / Steven Bleicher.-- 1st ed.
    p. cm.
  ISBN 1-4018-3740-9
  1. Color in art. 2. Color in design. 3. Color. I. Title: Contemporary color theory and use. II. Title.
  ND1488.B575 2004
  701'.85--dc22          2004007243

**NOTICE TO THE READER**

# Table of Contents

**Preface**

Color is the single most important design element. No other formal design component has its unique power. Color stimulates the eye and brain and creates an immediate unconscious response from the viewer. It can move the soul and sway emotions. It can physically affect the viewer's feelings of temperature, raise or lower pulse rate, blood pressure, and respiration, and make items appear lighter or heavier, near or far, cheap or expensive. The right color can make or break a work of art or design.

### Intended Audience

*Contemporary Color* has been developed and designed to teach the effective use of color across the areas of art and design. The text covers in detail fundamental studio elements along with a historical perspective to give the reader a deeper insight and understanding. The book has been designed with the awareness that artists and designers are visual learners. The pictures, images, and illustrations reinforce the text and bring the material to life. In addition, the book contains the most comprehensive and up-to-date information on color psychology.

Understanding the intrinsic power of color and its relationship with all of the other design elements is important for every artist, designer, and student. *Contemporary Color* may be used by both introductory and intermediate level art and design majors from community colleges to universities and professional art institutions and academies.

### Emerging Trends

Digital and other new technologies are now a part of every art and design student's education. It is vital that students understand them as well as they do traditional materials and methods of working with color. To this end, *Contemporary Color,* as its name suggests, also includes all forms of new technology, including digital imaging and animation, Web creations, virtual entities, lasers, and holography to prepare today's students for a future in art and design.

### Background of this Text

This book has been developed sequentially. Each chapter builds upon the information in the previous chapter to give the reader a complete understanding of this most complex of design elements. *Contemporary Color* bridges the areas of theory and practical application with its use of illustrations and professional examples from great design to outstanding works of art by emerging artists as well as modern masters.

While most books on color treat digital and other new forms of art as an afterthought, *Contemporary Color* integrates all forms of art throughout the text. This enables the reader to understand that these are not separate entities, but are all a part of the world of art and design. The theory and use of color is not handled one way on canvas and another on the computer; the same overriding principles apply for both. Only the medium changes, not the underlying concepts. Therefore, there has been a conscious effort to select images that span the scope of contemporary art and design.

In addition, the illustrations and images used in the text are predominantly contemporary art and design. I found throughout twenty years of being a practicing artist and teaching, that this approach makes much more sense to students—using examples of art and design they can relate to and that are a part of their lives. This allows a fresher perspective because students are not studying the distant past and trying to figure out how this might relate to what they are doing or may want to do. They are studying the recent past and present to understand how their contemporaries are using these concepts today.

This book was written to bring the material on color up to date not only in visual terms, but also in terms of the new philosophies, concepts, and media currently in use. The aim was to integrate all forms of contemporary art and design to show our common concerns and practices. This book is an attempt to bring sometimes divergent areas together, showing that with respect to color, we use one common language.

Since this book is solely about color, it is assumed that students have had some previous background in design. However, the text has been designed and developed to present the information in a clear, logical, and concise manner and to enable anyone to read and understand the materials, regardless of background.

## Textbook Organization

This book is organized and structured so that readers are introduced to the fundamental elements of color in a logical order. Each chapter builds on the previous one to give the reader a solid foundation, increasing their knowledge about and ability to use color effectively.

### Chapter 1: Color Perception

Color exists in and is as much a component of the function of the brain as it is the eye. This chapter explains the biology and physiology of vision, how a person sees and perceives color. It also presents an overview of the various modes of perception. Understanding how color is perceived is as important as how it can be used.

### Chapter 2: Color Theory—Making Sense of Color

From the dawn of time, mankind has tried to make sense of color. The theories that evolved have shaped our ideas and use of color. This chapter highlights the major theorists and their contributions, including contemporary theories of color from the palette to the swatch.

### Chapter 3: Color Psychology

We don't approach color in a vacuum. We carry with us a lifetime's worth of ideas, experiences, and preferences. These affect how we relate to color in everything from the products we buy, to the food we eat, to the color of our homes, to the clothes we wear, and they may even reveal aspects of our personality. Depending upon our age, sex, and socioeconomic background, our responses to color will vary accordingly. This chapter helps the artist and designer understand these issues in order to use color more effectively.

### Chapter 4: Color Harmonies

This chapter visually explains color harmonies, what they are, and why they are important to both artists and designers, as well as how to use them effectively. The full scope of color harmonies and their interactions are examined in a variety of media and styles.

### Chapter 5: Pigments, Colorants, and Paints

Not only is understanding color harmonies and their interactions necessary, but it is also equally vital to understand the composition of the materials or media used.

There are two types of colorants—traditional and digital. This chapter looks at traditional media including pigments, colorants, and dyes and explains their formulation and usage.

### Chapter 6: Digital Color

Today, learning about pigments is not enough. Nearly every image in any magazine, advertisement, product, and package has been digitally processed. It has become so much a part of our daily lives, we now take it for granted. This chapter explains digital color, from the most elemental level of the pixel to its complex digital elements.

### Chapter 7: Color and 3-D

The world we live in is not a two-dimensional space, though most of the art and designs created are two-dimensional. From sculpture to product design to new forms of dimensional art, color can be used to enhance or deny the dimensionality of a form or object. This chapter examines all aspects of color as it relates to working with forms and objects that are fully three-dimensional.

### Chapter 8: Color and Fine Art

Beginning with impressionism, this chapter reviews the trends and movements in modern art that have placed color at the forefront of their aesthetic philosophies. Pioneering movements from the Fauves, to expressionism, color-field painting, and op art are reviewed. Also, contemporary uses of color in environmental, installation, and conceptual art are examined.

### Chapter 9: Color and Design

Color is used to emphasize and accent a design or product and usually influences our buying decisions. This chapter shows how designers use color in graphics, advertising, packaging, industrial design, and animation to communicate their ideas effectively.

### Chapter 10: The Future of Color

Color doesn't stand still. It is always changing, developing, and transforming our lives. New technologies are allowing us to work with an ever-increasing array of colors and hues. This chapter examines new products, theories, concepts, and modes of expression. It also looks at the law and our legal system, one of the newest arbiters of color use.

## Features

The following list provides some of the salient features of the text:

- An innovative and contemporary approach to the introduction to color theory for students and a skill-sharpener for professionals.
- Equally focuses on traditional and digital color and their practical applications in contemporary art and design.
- Integrates digital and other new forms of art throughout the text.
- Clear, concise illustrations and images are used to supplement the text and encourage visual learning.
- Includes a comprehensive segment on the psychology of color.
- Color and 3-D are thoroughly explored, including types of media, colorants, and their uses.
- Colorants and pigments are examined to assist the artist and designer in choosing and using the correct medium to convey the concept or idea in the most effective manner possible.

## E-Resource

This guide on CD was developed to assist instructors in planning and implementing their instructional programs. It includes sample syllabi for using this book for either an 11- or 15-week semester. It also provides chapter review questions and answers, comprehensive studio exercises, and assignments. PowerPoint slides that highlight the main topics are an additional instructor resource. The CD also contains a bibliography of other supplemental books on color for further reading.

ISBN: 1401837425

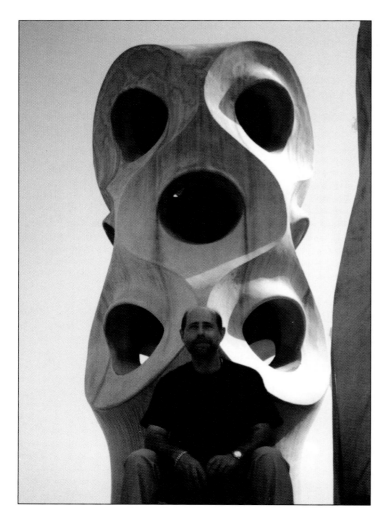

Steven Bleicher, sitting in front of sculptures on the rooftop garden of Antonio Gaudi's Casa Mila in Barcelona, Spain.

## About the Author

Steven Bleicher is a faculty member in the Arts and Humanities Program at the Art Institute of Fort Lauderdale. He received both his Bachelor of Fine Arts and Master of Fine Arts degrees from Pratt Institute in New York. Steven has worked and taught at the New York Studio School of Drawing, Painting and Sculpture, the State University of New York, Brooklyn College, and Marian College, in addition to serving as the Assistant Dean of the School of Art and Design at the Fashion Institute of Technology. He is a member of the College Art Association's Education Committee and is the Associate Editor of *FATE in Review*, the journal of Foundations in Art Theory in Education. He serves as an educational consultant in foundation curriculum and program design. In addition, Steven has presented papers and lectured on his innovative approaches to foundation studies and art education throughout the United States, Canada, and Europe.

Most recently, Steven has been developing a new book on Color Psychology. In conjunction with this effort he has become a highly sought-after consultant working with industry and speaking at colleges, universities, and professional organizations.

Steven is also an accomplished artist whose work is included in many major collections. His artwork is widely exhibited both nationally and internationally in numerous solo and group exhibitions. His artwork has also been reproduced in several books on art and design, and his approach to the artistic creative process was featured in Robin Landa's book, *The Creative Jolt*.

## Acknowledgments

Anne Majusiak deserves a very special thank you. As my picture researcher, it was through her diligent and tireless efforts that most of the images and their reproduction rights were acquired. She worked to secure all of the exact images I wanted, even though some were quite obscure and hard to find. It was an absolute pleasure working with her. Thanks, Anne.

I would like to thank all of the artists, designers, and others who freely contributed their work to this book. Your work is what this book is all about.

I would like to thank Robin Landa who suggested to Jim Gish and the editors at Delmar that I should be approached to write a book on color.

My appreciation and thanks also go out to Jim Gish and Jaimie Wetzel, my editors at Delmar, for all of their patience, support, and direction. In addition, I would like to thank the rest of the professional staff at Delmar, including Thomas Stover, production editor; Rachel Baker, art and design specialist; and Marissa Maiella, editorial assistant, who have made this book a reality.

I would also like to thank all my students and my colleagues' students who volunteered their work for the instructor's CD.

And lastly, a very special thank you to Helaine Cohn for her assistance, ideas, and encouragement.

Delmar Learning and the author would also like to thank the following reviewers for their valuable suggestions and expertise:

Ann Critchfield
Graphic Design Department
Art Institute of Atlanta
Atlanta, Georgia

Patricia Evans
Fine, Performing and Media Arts
Broome Community College
Binghamton, New York

Amanda Farrar
Graphic Design Department
Art Institute of Las Vegas
Henderson, Nevada

Ellen Goldstein
Accessories Design Department
Fashion Institute of Technology
New York, New York

Pam Hacker
Interior Design Program
Central Piedmont Community College
Charlotte, North Carolina

Bonnie Mitchell
Art Department
Bowling Green State University
Bowling Green, Ohio

Camille Murphy
Digital Media Department
Katherine Gibbs School
New York, New York

Barbara Pohl
Visual Communications and Digital Media Department
Katherine Gibbs School
New York, New York

Patrick Shuck
Art Department
St. Louis Community College—Meramac
Kirkwood, Missouri

Mark Snyder
Graphic Communications Department
Clemson University
Clemson, South Carolina

Anne Vaccaro
Art Department
Edison Community College
Piqua, Ohio

*Steven Bleicher*
*2004*

### Questions and Feedback

Delmar Learning and the author welcome your questions and feedback. If you have suggestions that you think others would benefit from, please let us know and we will try to include them in the next edition.

To send us your questions and/or feedback, you can contact the publisher at:

Delmar Learning
Executive Woods
5 Maxwell Drive
Clifton Park, NY 12065
Attn: Graphic Arts Team
800-998-7498

Or the author at:
Art Institute of Fort Lauderdale
Arts and Humanities Program
1799 SE 17th Street
Fort Lauderdale, FL 33316
stbleicher@aol.com

## Introduction

At the start of every term, I open up the windows and ask my class to look at the trees that cover our campus. I ask them what colors they see. I usually receive one response—green. I ask them to look again at the trees, at every leaf and write down every single color or aspect of the color they can see. The responses I get the second time around are much more varied. This is an exercise in sensitizing their eyes to color, to really see all of the color that is there. I want them to see the variation of greens that are there. I want them to realize just how many different greens there can be and the infinite variety of hues. This is the majesty and poetry of color.

Color is, in some sense, most closely related to music. They both have rhythm and harmony and are used to add emphasis and feeling. They can play directly on our senses and emotions and bypass our conscious minds, or they can be used for purely intellectual pursuits. There is a poetic aspect to each that can be hard to define. The goal of this book is to give the reader an understanding of color and an approach to such an ephemeral subject.

Our physiology, religious background, cultural heritage, and personal inclination determine our sense of color. Perceptual, psychological, and pictorial concerns can also affect the way we choose and work with color. Understanding how these elements influence our judgments and choices allows us, as artists and designers, to use them more effectively.

This book sets out to address all of these issues in a friendly, open manner. I have tried to write the book in the same way that I speak to my students—using a positive and upbeat approach—to pass on my excitement, enthusiasm, and passion for the subject. My hope is that you will learn to appreciate the tremendous variety, power, and sheer sensuous pleasure that is created with color.

**Dedication**

To my mother and father, who always
believed in me, and instilled the positive
attitude that I could accomplish whatever
I set out to do.

**Color Perception: Chapter 1**

Color is not real. It changes, fluctuates, and is transitory by its very nature. Color is poetry.

Why do we study color? Why is it important? Color may be the most underrated of all of the fundamental elements of design and yet it may be the most important and powerful. A single patch of color can communicate more than words themselves. A single hue can represent joy or sadness.

Color is one of only two design elements that produces an unconscious response from the viewer's brain (the other is texture). Viewers will respond to a specific color before they can read a label or make sense of the imagery. This is the power of color.

More has been written on imagery than color, because it is the most elusive and enigmatic of all of the elements of design. There are no absolutes. This is why many schools separate color from the other parts of design in their curriculum. A work of art can be about color alone (Figure 1-1) without having any specific imagery, as in the work of Dan Christensen.

Philosophers have said that the world is colorless and that our perceptions of hues are nothing more than illusions. This resembles the old question: if a tree falls in the woods and no one is around to hear it, does it still make a sound? You could ask a similar

**Figure 1-1.**
Dan Christensen,
*Untitled*, 1968.
© Dan Christensen,
Licensed by VAGA,
New York, NY.
Acrylic on Canvas.
(Courtesy of the artist.)
An artwork does not
have to have a specific
subject matter. It can be
realistic, abstract, or it
can be solely about color
and the application of
color. Christensen creates
bands of color that
appear to be in motion
and that captivate us with
their rich, intense hues.

question about color. If you close your eyes, does the world retain its color, or is it only in the eye of the beholder?

We can never know if our friend or neighbor sees exactly the same color in exactly the same way as we do. Color is a uniquely personal experience. This is another of color's mysteries. We can compare our thoughts and feelings, but as yet there is no measurable objective way to get a definitive answer. Standards are hard to come by. The most we can do is mix color by a specific formula to achieve a standardized result, but the perception of the hue is as varied as the shapes of snowflakes on a winter's day.

Color is a part of our daily life. Everything within our world is comprised of color, even though we take it for granted and never give it a second thought. The human eye and brain are marvelous organs—they allow us to experience our surroundings and take pleasure in this experience. Color can be enjoyed for its own sake. When we sit and look at a sunset, we are drawn by the magic of nature's palette. But this ability to revel in the beauty of a sunset is a uniquely human experience.

## Do Animals See Color?

Relatively few animals have the ability to see color in the same way we can.

Many use other means of perceiving their environment, including the ability to see infrared wavelengths of color that are invisible to humans. Among those that can see color are the higher primates, and new data suggests that dolphins and whales may also be able to see color. Most pets such as your dog and cat cannot see color. They see only shades of gray. So that bright yellow bone or pink-squeak toy are nothing more than shades of light gray to Fido. In the same way, your cat is not reacting to the color of the toy mouse, but is more likely reacting to the catnip imbedded in the toy (Figure 1-2). In our human zeal and love for our pets, we imbue them with our own characteristics and traits that they could not physiologically possess. As research continues, new information regarding how animals perceive their environment is being discovered. This knowledge adds to our own understanding of the sense of sight and color vision.

## Color Perception

We must understand how we see color before we can use it effectively. A better word may be *perceive* rather than *see*, because we do more that just observe color. How we perceive it—feel it, sense it, taste it, and are

**Figure 1-2.**
The image on the right is what you see—a brightly colored cat toy mouse. The image on the left is what your cat (or dog) would see. The color is for the owner and not the pet. The cat notices and may be drawn to the areas of high contrast, but it is the catnip inside that may be the real lure.

influenced by its ways—is still not completely understood. We are just beginning to scratch at the surface of this most powerful of all of the design elements.

The first step in sight and color perception is the response to the visual stimulus of light. This response or reaction to a stimulus is known as **sensation**—to the activation of light receptors that are the basic foundations of perception. **Perception** is the attempt to understand and make sense of the stimuli received. It does us no good to respond in some fashion if we don't understand what the stimulus is. The scientific term for the minimum amount of stimulus energy needed for perception is **absolute threshold**. In terms of sight, the minimum amount of light required to produce a visual entity is a candle flame at 30 miles on a clear night. While we would not be able to see any color from this distance, we would be able to perceive the light. Therefore, our visual acuity is much greater than we might initially imagine.

### Light and Color

Without light, there would be no vision or color, because light and color are inseparable. Light is considered visible energy. To make matters more complex, as the amount of light varies (increasing or decreasing), so does the amount of color. The images in Figure 1-3 show a landscape at different times during the same day. Notice that the color is not constant, but changes with the varying amount of light throughout the day. As the type of light changes from sunlight to artificial light, the quality of the color will also change. This total inconsistency of color makes it one of the most intriguing, poetic, and transitory elements to work with.

To fully understand this concept, pick a spot outside your window and look at a tree or any other object on a daily basis. Look at this item every day, at different times of the

day from morning, noon, and evening and watch how the color changes. This item that you thought was consistent in hue, value, and intensity is not—it changes as the amount and quality of light varies. For a more immediate example, just turn off the lights in the room you are in. You will see that as the amount of light changes, so does the color of everything in the room.

What we are really seeing when we look at color is the action and reaction of light. White light, or the visible spectrum, is composed of wavelength, amplitude, and saturation. This may also be referred to as visual stimulus. Wavelengths, the length of light waves, are measured in nanometers. The shorter wavelengths include X-rays and the visual spectrum of color and white light; the longest lengths include infrared, as seen in Figure 1-4. Different wavelengths are also associated with different hues. Shorter wavelengths indicate violet and blue, and longer wavelengths indicate yellows, oranges, and reds.

### Newton's Theory of Color

Sir Isaac Newton was one of the first to understand what we now consider our modern concept of the relationship of light and color. His experiments in the seventeenth century using a prism demonstrated that white light contained or was composed of the visible colors of the spectrum.

As shown in Figure 1-5, when white light enters the prism, it is refracted or bent as it comes out the other side, and the visible spectrum of colors is displayed.

The spectrum can also be seen as part of a naturally occurring event in a rainbow (Figure 1-6). The raindrops act in the same manner as a prism refracting and bending the light to create a multicolored arc. Newton devised that the spectrum was composed of seven separate, discernible hues. The acronym ROYGBIV that most of us learned in kindergarten stands for these: red,

**Figure 1-3.**
Notice how the color changes in the landscape at different times of the day as the amount and quality of the light changes. Top row: 7 a.m. and 9 a.m.; middle row: noon and 2 p.m.; bottom row: 5 p.m. and 6:30 p.m.

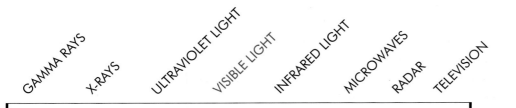

GAMMA RAYS   X-RAYS   ULTRAVIOLET LIGHT   VISIBLE LIGHT   INFRARED LIGHT   MICROWAVES   RADAR   TELEVISION

**Figure 1-4.**
A diagram illustrating the electromagnetic spectrum. We can only see a small portion of the entire spectrum. Some animals and insects can see infrared color wavelengths.

**Figure 1-5.**
An illustration of Newton's principle of white light being broken down into the colors of the spectrum after it passes through a prism.

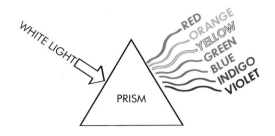

**Figure 1-6.**
A rainbow is created when light hits the falling raindrops and is refracted like a prism. Newton may have been inspired by these natural events. The colors of a rainbow are the same spectral hues produced by a prism.

orange, yellow, green, blue, indigo, and violet. However, most people can only discern six of these hues; they have trouble telling the difference between indigo and violet.

It has been surmised that either Newton had great color acuity and could see a wider range of colors than the majority of people, or that he picked the number seven since it is considered a holy number. We must remember that, previously, Newton got into a great deal of trouble with the authorities and church with his earlier theories of gravity and was imprisoned for a time. So, this may have

been his way of ameliorating his past transgressions with the church and thereby avoiding prison again.

## Sources of Light

When we look at an apple and observe its bright red color, what we are seeing are the reflected lightwaves. There are two parts that make up a reflection or the bouncing of light waves from a given surface (Figure 1-7). The **incident beam** comes from the light source hitting the object. The **reflected beam** bounces off the object and allows us to see its particular hue. When the surface is smooth, these lightwaves bounce off or are reflected in an even manner. With a rough surface, the reflected beams bounce off and are scattered in many different directions.

Another factor in determining color is the light source used to view any given object. Different light sources will affect the color perceived. The best light source is sunlight because it is the most accurate in color reproduction. While you can get light bulbs that equal the brightness and intensity of sunlight, they tend to be very expensive, last only a few hours, and burn very hot which can cause injury. When speaking about traditional light bulbs, they are more correctly referred to as lamps. A light fixture is actually called a **luminaire**, although the term has fallen out of common usage. There are several types of lamps, including neon, tungsten, fluorescent, and halogen. Halogen lights are most commonly used in automobile headlamps because they

**Figure 1-7.**
As white light hits the orange, all of the spectral hues are absorbed except for the orange hue, which is reflected, giving the fruit its color and name.

give off a very bright light that can illuminate a large area. By far the most widely used lamps are fluorescent and tungsten. They are used in both home and industry and offer the best in affordability, ease of operation, and overall illumination. All bulbs or lamps are sources of radiant light, which means that the light is directly emitted from an energy source. The other sources of radiant light are the sun, lamps of all types, and other hot objects. Reflected light is the light cast back and is caused by the light waves bouncing off an object.

## Metamerism

Since there are so many different types of lamps and light sources, understanding their effect on color perception is essential. Tungsten, or incandescent bulbs, tend to give off a warm light and bring out the warmer range of hues including yellows, oranges, and reds. Fluorescent lights, on the other hand, burn much cooler and create a cool cast to objects by bringing out a greater range of green, blue, and violet hues. Therefore, an object may appear to be one shade of a hue under one type of lamp and look drastically different when viewed with another light source (Figure 1-8). This occurrence is called **metamerism**. Many art students learn firsthand about this phenomenon when they complete a color assignment at home, normally under incandescent light, and then bring their work to class where it is usually viewed under fluorescent light. The resulting shift in value and intensity in their projects causes frustration and concern among students and grading nightmares for their instructors. In many cases, students and teachers must agree in advance which light source should be used to create and then view the color assignments. Only then can consistent results be achieved.

SUNLIGHT    TUNGSTEN LIGHT

## The Human Eye

Now that we understand how light affects color, the other major factor in perceiving color is the eye. While the eye has often been referred to as a camera, it is much more than that. It is a very complex receptor that sends its information as electrical impulses to the brain, which in turn makes sense of these various stimuli. The brain interprets the data sent to it and in many respects the visual images and colors we see are really a function of the mind and not the eye.

The human eye is actually a receptor for light. Light passes through the cornea, which helps to focus the light waves (Figure 1-9). It also functions as a protective covering.

**Figure 1-8.**
An example illustrating the concept of metamerism. As the type of light changes from daylight to tungsten light, the quality of the hue perceived changes. The sunlight makes the hue appear to be lighter and more saturated.

**Figure 1-9.**
A diagram of a cross-section of the human eye. Light enters the pupil and hits the retina at the back of the eye, which contains the rods and cones. These photo-receptors translate light into electrical impulses. This information is transmitted to the brain via the optic nerve.

The light then passes through the aqueous humor, a fluidlike substance that supplies nourishment to the organ, and continues through the lens, finally striking the retina. Located in the back of the eye, the retina has several layers of cells that are specialized to interpret different aspects of this incoming data. These visual receptors make up the photoreceptor layer, which includes the rods and cones.

### Rods and Cones

Rods and cones are aptly named due to their specific shapes (Figure 1-10). Rods are long, thin, and cylindrically shaped. Their sole purpose is to read lights and darks, or value. They cannot perceive color at all. This is why as something comes into your field of vision, you make out its shape long before you can make out its color. The rods can operate in extremely low light, which is many hundred times less than the cones. Cones are fat, bulgy-shaped receptors that

perceive color. They require much more light to process information. Some feel that because they require much more light to process color, that this is the reason we see so little color at night. Another reason, we understand, is that the greater the amount of light, the brighter the color that can been seen. Therefore, it makes perfect sense that at night when there is so little light, we would only be able to perceive small amounts of color, regardless of physiology. It becomes another question of which came first—the chicken or the egg. Is it because the cones need more light to process information that we see very little color at night, or is it because it is dark and with less light very little if any color can be seen?

In total, there are more than 100 million rods and only about 6 million cones in each eye. The rods and cones are massed together in three groups. The first group is composed of all rods, the next is a combination of rods and cones, and the last group is made up only of cones. This area comprised of only cones is found in the **fovea**, a depressed spot in the center of the retina. To put this into perspective, the fovea contains 350,000 cones and is smaller than the head of a pin. Because of this, we only see color as a very small area of our field of vision. The area of the highest color acuity is only about a two-degree area directly in front of our vision field. Subconsciously our eyes zoom in on this area when we want to examine the color of an area or object.

Located just below the fovea is the optic nerve, which consists mainly of fibers derived from the ganglionic cells of the retina. It carries the information from the eye to the brain where it is converted to the images we see. At the point where the optic nerve passes through the optic disk, there is a hole in the retina where there are no photoreceptors. Consequently, the brain receives no visual information from this area of vision. This area

**Figure 1-10.**
A diagram illustrating the rods and cones that are actual photo-receptors in the retina. Rods are long and thin, and cones are bulgy. Light activates the light-sensitive pigments in the rods and cones.

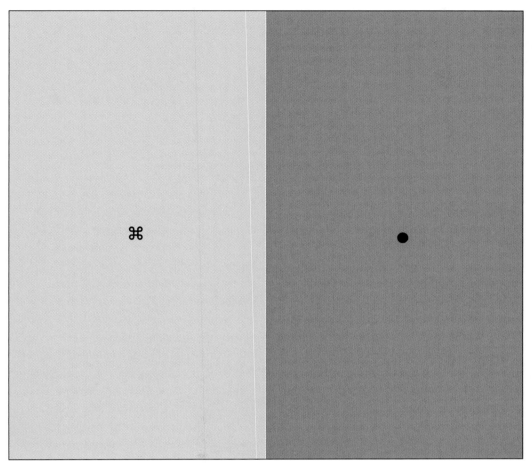

**Figure 1-11.**
Finding your blind spot. Hold the book up at arm's length. Keep your left eye closed and look at the four-leaf-clover-shaped squiggle. As you move the book toward yourself, you will find that the spot on the magenta background has disappeared. You have just found your blind spot. Flip the book over and close your right eye this time to find your other blind spot. Everyone has two—one for each eye.

is your "blind spot." Actually you have two, one in each eye. This area is fairly large, as you can see in the illustration in Figure 1-11.

Even today, scientists are not completely sure how cones work. They contain a light-sensitive pigment called **iodopsin.** While much of how the iodopsin works is still not known, it's believed that there are three types of cone pigment each for sensing a different wavelength of light: blue-violet for short range, green for middle range, and red for the longest wavelengths. This generally accepted theory is known as the **trichromatic theory,** but much research must still be done to know for sure.

Rods also contain a light-sensitive pigment called visual purple or **rhodopsin.** As light hits this pigment, it burns or bleaches it, and thereby changing the electrosignal for

darkness transmitted by the rods to the brain. In low light, rods have very high amounts of unbleached visual purple. This allows us to see in these conditions.

## Afterimages

Another theory of color vision states that cones are grouped together in pairs: red with green and blue with orange, and so on. As one fires off, the other is inhibited or stopped from firing. This **opponent–process theory** accounts for color processing in the bipolar cells and thalamus. But this process is important to us because it may be responsible for color afterimages. Color **afterimage** is the perception of a color that isn't really there and is seen as the complement of the color being viewed. Seeing an afterimage can make many people dizzy and sick.

**Figure 1-12.**
Stare at the red airplane for at least 30 seconds. Then quickly turn your gaze to the black dot. What do you see? This is an afterimage.

Look at the red airplane in Figure 1-12. Stare at it for a minute or so, then look at the black dot next to it. You will see a green afterimage. This is why all hospital operating theaters are painted a pale green. Think about a surgeon performing an operation staring into an open body cavity filled with blood. As the surgeon looks up, he would see green spots which could make him nauseous or feel ill, which is the last thing a patient would want a surgeon to feel in the middle of a procedure! But the spots are mitigated by the light green hue of the walls. Remember, you must have some of the color's complement to relieve afterimage.

**Color Perception Deficiencies**

There are many things that can affect color perception. These can include accidents and injuries, aging, disease, drug use, or even heredity. A physiologic response, but one not so easily remedied, is color blindness. There are only a very few people who are truly color blind and we call them **monochromatics**. These people have only one type of cone: it treats all wavelengths of light the same and sends the brain faulty information, so that they only perceive shades of gray. If you want to experience this condition, dim the lights in a room until you can no longer see any hues, just shades.

The more apt name used for people who suffer some form of color insufficiency is color deficiency. The Ishihara Color Test (Figure 1-13) is the diagnostic tool used to test color deficiency and diagnose specific insufficiencies. The most common color deficiency is dichromatic, or the inability

**Figure 1-13.**
An example of one of the plates from the Ishihara Color Test. What number do you see? If you do not see a number, you may want to have yourself tested to see if you have a color deficiency.

to see one of the three primary colors (Figure 1-14). The person lacks one type of cone and therefore has problems seeing opponent colors such as red and green, or blue and yellow. Most commonly found in men, it's believed that there is a genetic or hereditary basis. It is estimated that 7 percent of the men in America, or nearly 10 million men, are color deficient, while only .04 percent of women are affected.

Certain physical ailments such as diabetes and vitamin B12 deficiencies can also affect the lens and impair color vision. As people age, the lens can also yellow and thereby decrease the ability to discern hues. This can lead to color confusion, and with so many elderly people taking several medications on a daily basis, this condition could be life threatening. In a study in 1984, Peter Hurd and Julia Blevins found that many senior citizens with these conditions experienced difficulties in differentiating between blue and green capsules, as well as many shades of green and yellow. This has led to many instances of people mistaking medications and taking the wrong prescription, which caused serious complications.

Recently, however, there have been remarkable advances in correcting color deficiencies. There are now a few companies making corrective lenses and even one company that makes a Web-browsing utility. ColorMax offers a specialized lens that reflects the light waves in such a way as to compensate for the color deficiency. A company called Solarguard makes sunglasses that not only filter out harmful ultraviolet rays, but also aid in color correction. The newest technology developed by a software manufacturer is a product that adjusts the color on your monitor to compensate for color perception deficiencies. With these and other recent advancements, color insufficiencies are no longer the problem they once were and may one day be a thing of the past.

**Synesthesia**

Another form of color perception is **synesthesia.** Synesthetes, people who have this perception abnormality, perceive their environment by using a peculiar combination of two or more senses to understand and relate to the world around them. For them, sounds have color, shapes may have flavors, and scents may have color counterparts. This is not a metaphoric relation, but a true and real way of experiencing the world. For example, a synesthete would not see the letters on this page in black and white, but in color, as pictured in Figure 1-15.

There are three basic types of synesthesia: developmental, which starts in early child-hood and is not learned, but an involuntary response; acquired, which may occur as a result of a tumor, injury, or accident; and drug induced, caused by taking LSD or another hallucinogenic drug. The main differences

**Figure 1-14.**
In this split image, the picture on the left is how a person with normal color vision would see the four brightly colored rubber balls. The picture on the right is what the same scene would look like to someone with a red-green color deficiency, which is the most common form of color insufficiency.

**Figure 1-15.**
An example of how a synesthete would see a page of text. Synesthetes see each letter as a separate hue for a total of twenty-six different color variations, one for each letter.

This is not a metaphoric relation but a true and real way of experiencing their world.

between these three types are that in both the acquired and drug-induced states, the resulting visualizations are unorganized and random. For example, if a developmental (or true) synesthete sees the letter R as red, they will always see it as red. Their visualizations are constant and never vary.

Artists and designers have long been interested in this form of perception and have tried to use it as a means of enhancing their sensory awareness and artistic sense. One exercise regularly used by many artists and

teachers is to play a piece of music and have listeners draw or paint the feelings they experience. There are many such examples of this, including David Hockney's *Ravel's Garden with NightGlow* and Wassily Kandinsky's *Impression III*. Hockney listened to Maurice Ravel's music and painted his impressions by trying to approximate the synesthesic experience. *Impression III* (Figure 1-16) was painted a few days after Kandinsky attended a Schoenberg New Year's concert in Munich. Inspired by the

**Figure 1-16.**
Wassily Kandinsky, *Impressions III (Concert)*, 1911. ©2004 Artists Rights Society (ARS), New York/ADAGP, Paris. Kandinsky often listened to music as a means of inspiration for his paintings. The color and images in this painting were Kandinsky's interpretation of the music he heard at a concert. He wanted to capture in paint the feeling of the music.

atonal music, the black area relates to the top of a grand piano juxtaposed to the large yellow mass, which may be reminiscent of the lighted stage. The two white columns help stabilize the composition's diagonal elements. Probably the most famous artist who tried to combine the concept of art and music was Walt Disney in the movie *Fantasia*. Disney took several classical pieces of music and animated them to combine the viewer's senses and bring the music to life. This was his attempt to allow viewers to see the music and hear with their eyes.

Our contemporary concept of multimedia is an attempt to combine both sound and visuals to express an idea, convey a message, or even sell a product. Virtual realities also rely on the use of multiple sensory inputs to allow users to suspend their sense of what is real and accept the illusions set before them. Scientists have also discovered that people make a better connection to material when more than one sense is involved or stimulated. By combining auditory and visual stimuli, the brain produces more synaptic pathways that create solid links to the material and make it easier to recall when tested. Music videos are another form of the application of this concept. The aim of a music video is to visualize the lyrics, mood, and melody of the song and to enhance the listener's appreciation and enjoyment.

### Color and Health

Color and light have long been known to possess healing qualities. While not thoroughly understood, they have been used in both traditional medicine and alternative therapies. For example, hospitals use phototherapy on infants born prematurely who often suffer from jaundice. This and other forms of light and color therapies are used in treating dermatological ailments including psoriasis and acne. Researchers at Cornell University reported that applying

blue light to the back of the knees can reset the body's internal clock and alleviate sleep disturbances that accompany shift work. New areas including the use of these treatments for AIDS-related tumors are also being explored.

In clinical studies, an Italian physician, Dr. Ponza, painted rooms (including their windows) one hue so that the occupants were literally bathed with colored light. For example, it was found that when patients were placed in a green room, their capillaries dilated. On the other hand, red increased muscle tone and had a stimulating effect. But the most striking conclusion from these studies was that the colored environments had an effect on both sighted and blind patients. The blind participants were affected in the exact same manner as the sighted. When a blind person was placed in a green room, even though there was no way they could "see" the color, their blood vessels also dilated in the same way and to the same degree as the sighted patient. When the blind patient was moved to a room with another hue, they responded in the same manner as the other patients. This lead to the conclusion that there must be other color receptors in the body. While experiments of this type have been repeated with similar results, it is still a mystery as to the location and physiology of these color receptors.

Another area of study on alternative color perception is known as **dermo-optic** vision. In this form of perception, the person quite literally feels the color. There have been a number of theories regarding how it works, including the hypothesis that there are sensors in the skin that pick up the energy field or wavelengths of the color. It has been noted that the ability to detect colors by touch increases under bright light and decreases in low light. This is the same as our ability to see color with our eyes: the less light, the more limited range of hues we

**Figure 1-17.**
A Kirlian photograph of a fingertip showing the person's aura. Some people believe that all things, animate, and even inanimate objects, have auras. These electromagnetic fields are made up of the same energy as light waves and produce the colors seen in the photograph. (Photograph courtesy of Jerry Muehe.)

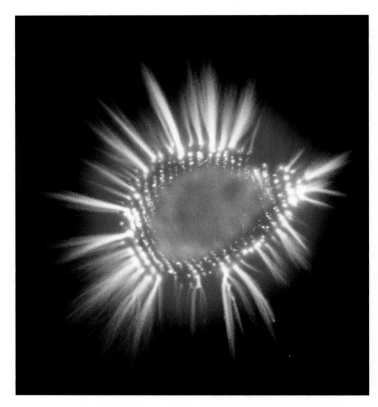

are able to distinguish. Another interesting side note was that respondents sensed warm and cool hues in much the same manner as sighted people respond to color temperature. This may suggest that this aspect of color perception may be more innate and depends more on biology than environment or education.

### Chromatherapy

Chromatherapy is another use of color; it is the science of healing with colors. This treatment can range from bathing patients in colored light to having them meditate on a specific hue. Kirlian photography, named after its inventor, is a photographic process in which a current is passed through an object (or person) and the corona or discharge is recorded onto film. The exposed paper shows the electromagnetic field and glowing aura of the subject. It is believed that the auras correspond to the seven major energy centers or "chakras" in the body and can be read to diagnose certain ailments or even one's spiritual equilibrium. Figure 1-17 shows a Kirlian photograph of the tip of a finger. The red and blue aura radiates out from the orange center, or fingertip, and the white lines show that the electromagnetic field is present.

Some believe that this aura exists in everyone and everything and is the energy field within all physical objects. This electromagnetic field produces a variety of colors, where red is considered the densest and follows the sequence of the spectrum to violet, which is said to have the highest frequency. The size, shape, and colors displayed in the image will vary from individual to individual.

There are eight colors normally used in chromatherapy. They include white and the seven spectral hues. It is believed that each has their own special healing properties.

White—contains all of the colors in the spectrum and is used to relax and soothe.

**Red**—enhances energy and stimulates the production of red blood cells.

Orange—increases sexual stimulation and increases pleasure. It also represents youth and curiosity.

Yellow—may have antibacterial properties, and is associated with wisdom and clarity.

**Green**—used to treat bacterial infections and in healing stomach ulcers. It is also considered calming and since it is also in the exact middle of the spectrum, it brings balance to the individual.

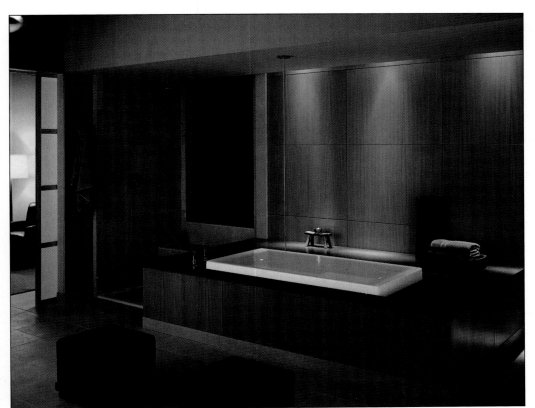

**Figure 1-18.**
Kohler Chromatherapy tub with magenta light. An example of Kohler's new line of chroma-therapy bathtubs. The bather is immersed in water and colored light to help relieve stress, creating a unique bathing experience.

**Blue**—decreases toxins in the body and is said to promote knowledge and self-assuredness.

**Indigo**—aids in intuition, inspiring the individual. It also has a sedative effect.

**Violet**—is used for calming the nervous system and promoting creativity and spiritual awakening.

Many companies have jumped on the chromatherapy bandwagon. Kohler, a major manufacturer of kitchen and bath fixtures, offers a line of tubs that includes a color-therapy feature (Figure 1-18). This allows the bather to be totally immersed in a combination of colored water and light. "By enhancing the bathing experience with chromatherapy, Kohler has created a welcome refuge within the home, away from our stress-laden, busy lives," said Michael Moldenhauer, marketing manager of bathing products for Kohler. "Again, we are trying to raise the bar on what embodies the ultimate bathing ritual."

## Luminotherapy

Even white light can have a therapeutic effect. Seasonal affective disorder, or SAD, produces anxiety and depression in some people who live in areas with little natural sunlight during the winter months. Lumino-therapy, or the use of lights with the same photosensitivity as sunlight (about 55,000 K) has proven to be an effective treatment. The patient is required to sit in front of the special lamps for 30 minutes or more, usually on a daily basis. The light stimulates the pineal gland and increases the production of melatonin, a hormone involved in regulating the body's internal clock. Melatonin is also an antioxidant, which may also increase the body's ability to fight infection and disease.

The field of color therapies and other uses of color and light as healing agents is still at an infancy in Western medicine. Eastern traditions have long accepted the role of color in a person's well-being and

**Figure 1-19.**
In the Feng Shui compass, north is at the bottom and south is at the top. Each color relates to a force of nature, just as some of the early color theories that will be studied in the following chapter.

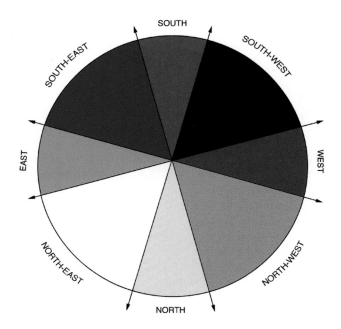

continued health. Practitioners of Feng Shui use various hues in the home and workplace to produce an optimum balance of the energy forces. In Figure 1-19, the hues of the Feng Shui compass show the eight types of "chi"—the subtle flow of electromagnetic energy, which is said to exist in everything and link the universe. The colors of the compass also correspond to the time of day, season of the year, and birth order, as well as parts of the body. What role these various color and light therapies will play in the future is still under study, but one thing is certain— we are only now beginning to understand the healing and curative powers that are associated with color.

## Summary

Light is the basis for all color. For this reason, color and light are inseparable. The amount and quality of the light will determine the strength and brightness of the color we perceive. In the seventeenth century, Sir Isaac Newton demonstrated what we now consider to be our modern concept of the relationship of light and color—that white light contains all of the spectral hues. What we actually see is the reflected color of an object. Light, and therefore color, is captured by the photoreceptors in the eye and transmitted to the brain via the optic nerve. Therefore, we are discovering that the brain may be the real color perception organ.

There are many types of color perception, from dermo-optic vision, the concept that there are other color receptors in the body, to synesthesia, the concept that in some individuals two or more senses are needed to perceive and understand the world. All of these enhance the color experience and are used by artists and designers in the creative process. From auras and medical uses of light in luminotherapy, we are still exploring the ways in which our bodies perceive light and color. New scientific breakthroughs will continue to expand our notion of color.

**Color Theory–Making Sense of Color: Chapter 2**

**M**ankind has been trying to make sense of color and its use since the dawn of time. Our artist ancestors, the cave painters, used a limited range of hues made from natural elements to express representations and images of their world. For example, in the buffalo shield pictured in Figure 2-1, the red circles symbolize sun haloes— the circles that can be seen around the sun prior to a storm. The small black dashed lines represent pieces of the warrior so tiny that his enemies would not be able to harm him.

**Figure 2-1.**
Buffalo rawhide shield, four red circles.
© The Field Museum, #A111351c.
A Crow war shield made from buffalo hide. The symbols and colors used by each tribe represented their concepts of the meaning of color.

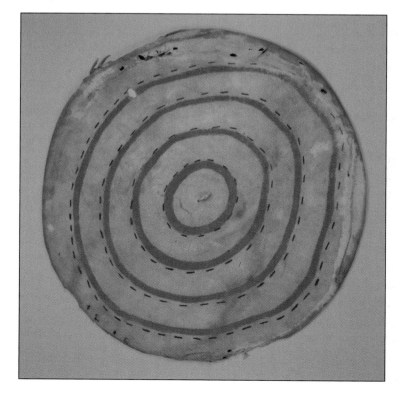

As far as we can tell, there was little thought as to how the various hues cave painters used related to each other and to their primitive world. Throughout time, each culture and tribal group have had their own various symbolic uses of color. However, it wasn't until Aristotle that thoughts of how colors were formed and how they might be used together in some harmonious way began to evolve. And they have been evolving and changing ever since. The one thing that can be said about color theory is that it is ever changing. As digital and other new technological applications are invented, our conception and thoughts about color will change with them.

Many early theories were highly subjective, with moral overtones. Others showed the personal bias of the author. They speculated on how and why we see the various hues around us. Color theories assist the artist and designer in finding a logical and reliable method of dealing with color. These theories also were developed to help communicate ideas about color to other artists, designers, and manufacturers. Moreover, they helped to answer the most basic questions about color— how it was formed and how it could be used. Theories changed as man's basic understanding of science and technology evolved. Even today, new theories of color in a digital or computational age are being addressed and rediscovered. But before we can understand where we may be going, it is important to know where we have been and how we arrived at our contemporary understanding of color.

Today, more is written about imagery than color. With the widespread use of digital and other new technologies in both fine art and design, there is a resurgence in theorizing about color and its role in new media and as a vehicle for communication. The field may be more wide open than ever with new developments taking place on an almost daily basis. No contemporary artist works from a single color theory. They can mix and match the best of all theories, using what works and discarding what does not.

## Naming Color

After the first six hues—red, blue, yellow, orange, green, and violet—there has been little agreement about the names for any given color. Names have more to do with language and culture than hue or chroma. Originally, names had to do with the pigment content of the paint. The names were descriptive of the minerals, plants, and other things that made up the colorants or pigments. As far back as the eighteenth century, hues still had simple direct names, such as sky blue, and primary yellow. During the nineteenth century and with the ever-increasing explorations and colonialism of the west, there was a shift that gave the various hues more romantic sounding names such as canary yellow, Tahitian green, and so on. But it was the boom of the 1950s and on that changed the naming of color. Hues took on descriptive names such as bubble gum pink and fire engine red. Colors were being named by manufacturers to boost the sales of their products. During the 1960s and 1970s, the names of colors became synonymous with commercialism and consumerism. When we think of names such as harvest gold or avocado, we automatically think of kitchen appliances including refrigerators and stoves. Color names are developed by an industry to fit their particular need. The names used by a cosmetics company would vary widely from the names given to hues used in the automotive industry. There is no uniformity or convention. Hue names keep changing with the times to reflect the culture and society and fads of the day.

## The Color Circle

Most color theories are based on a circular arrangement of the hues in a chromatic order or sequence. They may be viewed as a circle,

**Figure 2-2.**
Color is usually portrayed in a circular format as a wheel, sphere, or simple circle.

wheel, or sphere, as in Figure 2-2. This circular format allows relationships between each hue to be expressed in a concise visual manner. In this type of arrangement, each hue can be viewed individually or in relation to one another. The ring-shaped format also works the best for showing the relationships in subtractive color theory. There are several types or versions including additive, subtractive, process, and pigment-oriented color wheels. Philosophically, the circle represents a continuum: we don't think of color as ending, but being ongoing, so the circle adds to the poetic notion of color.

## Aristotle

Aristotle may be considered the grandfather of color theory by virtue of having written the first known book on the subject, *DeColoribus*. He wrote that all colors were derived from different mixtures of sunlight, firelight, air, and water (Figure 2-3). Blacks, as well as the darker hues, were a result of the lack of one or more of these elements. A dark shade of a hue, for example, might be caused by a unique combination of blackness and either sunlight or firelight as they mixed in the atmosphere. He developed these concepts based on observation and experience and

**Figure 2-3.**
Aristotle's color palette was based on natural phenomena. He believed that it was the combination of two or more of these elements that produced the colors we see.

believed this explained why we see fiery reds at dawn and dusk. His basic color palette included red, yellow, blue, green, and violet, as well as white, black, and brown. But in the end, he felt that art was really all about line and that all the rest, including color, was merely ornamental.

### da Vinci

Leonardo da Vinci was not only one of the most accomplished artists of his day, but he was also a scientist and inventor. His notebooks are filled with new inventions, such as the helicopter, and anatomical studies of cadavers. He brought these same powers of investigation and observation to color in his *Treatise on Painting* that was published posthumously in 1651, more than a hundred years after his death. He proposed a basic set of six hues, as seen in Figure 2-4. Each color held a direct relationship to the natural world. In his color set, white related to light, yellow stood for the earth, green for water, blue for air, red for fire, and black for night or darkness. As a highly religious person, these associations of hues to the natural world were a spiritual manifestation in paint of his devout convictions. It would not be for

another fifty years that the study of color would be treated in a scientific manner and that the influence of religion would not play a dominant role in its treatment.

### Newton

If Aristotle is the grandfather, then Newton surely must be considered the founding father of color theory. As we have seen previously, he was the first to bring a scientific method of investigation to the study of color. He endeavored to find a basic truth behind the nature and science of color. In his 1701 book, *Opticks*, he experimented with the defraction of light through a prism to devise a spectral color range of hues. He realized that the prism broke down the white light, showing the seven hues that make up the spectrum. He was also the first to place hues in a circular arrangement, a format that is still used today. Newton's color circle or wheel (Figure 2-5) is based on light and not pigment so that the center is white and indicates the combination or mixing of all the colors. A few years later, J.C. Le Blon would adopt much of his research in creating his own color ideology. It could be said that Newton laid the groundwork for all who

**Figure 2-4.**
A diagram illustrating da Vinci's color palette that was based on his religious convictions. Notice how each of the colors relates to a physical manifestation of the natural world.

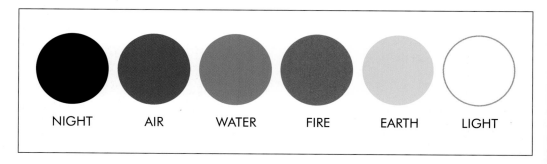

followed and that for the rest of time, theorists were either railing against or basing their work on his experiments.

### Le Blon and Harris

In 1703, J. C. Le Blon developed the theory of the primary color system. His concept was that three hues—yellow, red, and blue—could not be reduced or broken down any further and therefore were the primary or basic hues (Figure 2-6). He also stated that these hues could be mixed or blended in varying combinations to make up all of the other colors. From these studies, Le Blon developed the first four-color printing process, or subtractive color process, whose basic scheme of cyan, magenta, yellow, and black is still with us today.

More than fifty years later in 1766, Moses Harris, an English engraver, took Le Blon's primary pigment concept one step further. In his book, *The Natural System of Color,* Harris developed one of the first full-color circles, which spaced the primaries at equal distances from one another. He placed the primaries, or *primitives,* as he referred to them, at the very heart of the circle. Harris placed shades of each hue on the inner part of the circle and tints moving off from the pure hue to the outer edge of the circle with a total of eighteen hues in all.

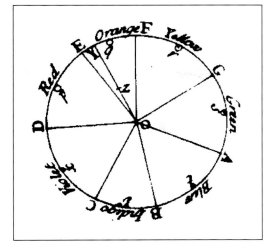

**Figure 2-5.**
A reproduction of Newton's color wheel containing seven hues, the colors of the spectrum that he saw as a result of his experiments with a prism. Notice that all of the color spaces are not equal in size.

### Goethe and Impressionism

As a poet and not a scientist, Johann Wolfgang von Goethe was more concerned with the subjective interpretation of color than an objective impartial examination of the subject. His work is very personal in nature, unlike Newton who tried to follow scientific methodology. Goethe tried to replicate Newton's prism experiment, but was shocked and very disappointed with the results. Expecting to have the entire wall covered or bathed in a multicolored rainbow of lights, he was angered to find only a thin strip of spectral color. He immediately decided that Newton was a fraud and spent his entire life berating Newton's ideas. All of Goethe's future work

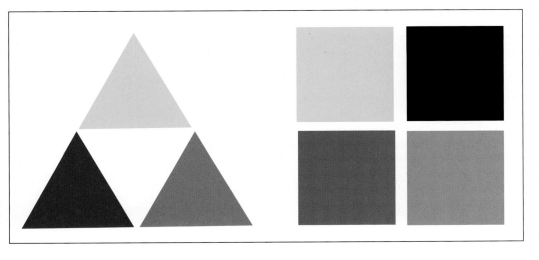

**Figure 2-6.**
Le Blon developed the concept of the primary hues of red, yellow, and blue and then modified this concept to come up with the primary hues of cyan, magenta, yellow, and black used in production printing. Cyan is a lighter form of blue and tends to mix better to give a wider range of colors. Magenta is related to red, but it creates brighter color when it is used to make secondary hues of orange and violet.

**Figure 2-7.**
An example of Goethe's color wheel in which all of the color spaces are equal in size. It was one of the first to show the relationships of hues to their complements.

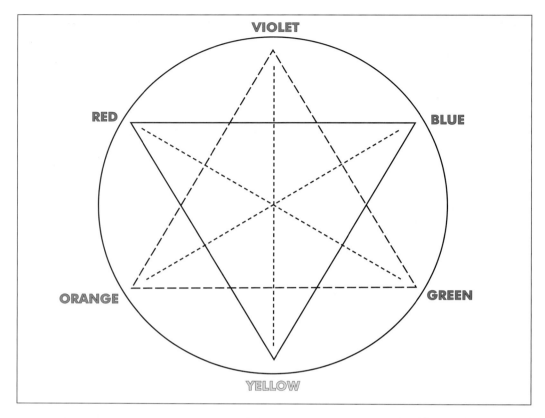

**Figure 2-8.**
Vincent Van Gogh. *Night (after Millet)*, 1889.
Courtesy of the Van Gogh Museum, Amsterdam (Vincent Van Gogh Foundation). Van Gogh read Goethe's color theory and used it in this painting to create the colored shadows. The blues in the shadows of the man are complementary to the oranges used in the figure. The lines of the shadows also act as a pictorial device to lead us into the center of the picture.

was the antithesis of Newton's and he never missed an opportunity to denigrate the scientist's work.

Goethe felt that color was really the function of the eye and not the sole property of light. He felt light should not be broken down, but viewed as a whole and studied not in the lab, but in the natural world. In his 1810 book, *Theory of Colors,* his writings focused on visual phenomena. He felt his mission was to bring order to the world of color (Figure 2-7). One of his major contributions was the examination of light hitting an object and the discovery that shadows were not always black or gray, but contained color. These colored shadows were comprised of color complements and were most often produced when the main light source was not pure bright white or when a secondary light source was involved. The Impressionists and the Postimpressionists read Goethe's writings. His influence on their work can be seen in many of their paintings in the colored shadows.

Dutch painter Vincent Van Gogh was especially influenced by Goethe's concept of colored shadows and applied it in several of his paintings. In *Night (after Millet)* (Figure 2-8), the painting is illuminated by the light in the background, which creates large cast shadows from the figures, extending out into the foreground. These blue shadows are full of color and are complementary to the orange attire of the seated male figure and the firelight.

Unfortunately Goethe's writings are biased and show his personal and subjective view of color. For example, he had a strong preference for warm hues over cool. He saw them as being exciting and, by contrast, cool hues as dull and lifeless. But his written work on color has outlasted his poetry and is still read and used by contemporary artists.

## Chevreul, Rood, and Pointillism

A contemporary of Goethe, Michel Eugene Chevreul was a French chemist and head of one of the leading dye houses in Paris. In his early work with dyes and colorants, he verified much of Moses Harris's work that all hues could be derived or created from the three primaries. He distinguished and described three main elements or attributes to color: purity (saturation), value (luminosity), and hue (Figure 2-9). But his major contribution was in developing color harmonies or color schemes. He wrote that two or more hues next to each other on the color wheel will optically blend and work with each other, and that strongly contrasting hues were placed opposite each other on the color wheel. While many of the Impressionists such as Monet rejected his ideas, these concepts were embraced by French painter, Georges Seurat and became central to his concept of visual color mixing.

**Figure 2-9.**
An illustration of Chevreul's basic concept of hue, purity, and value. The center circle shows the represented hue of green. The vertical axis represents purity or saturation with the most saturated version of the hue at the top and the most desaturated at the bottom. The horizontal axis represents value with the left side showing a tint of the middle color, and the far right side expressing a shade of the same hue.

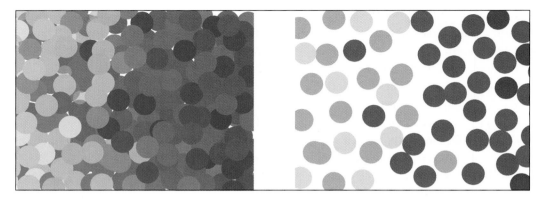

**Figure 2-10.**
An example of how the pointillist style of visual color mixing works. If the dots or dabs of color are touching one another, then the colors will blend in the viewer's eye. On the right you can see that when there is space between the dots, we read them as separate colors.

Another major influence on Seurat was the work of Ogden Rood. Rood was trained as both an artist and scientist. Using spinning disks, he proved that pigments could be optically or visually combined as the disks turned to simulate the effect of the mixing or blending lights. On a still plate or picture, the same effect could be achieved if dots or points of paint were very small and placed next to each other. The dots must be so close as to actually touch each other. Otherwise, if there was any space in between them, the eye would not visually mix the hues, but would read them as separate and distinct colors (Figure 2-10).

Seurat was the leading exponent of visual color mixing. He applied and used this theory as the basis of his pointillist style, as seen in Figure 2-11, *The Seine at Bourbevoic.*

Other artists including Camille Pissarro and Vincent Van Gogh also began using Rood's color concepts in their painting. But Rood was not flattered by their adoption of his theories. Quite the opposite, he was appalled at the way his theories were put in practice by Seurat and others. He once said to his son that if that was what he had contributed to modern art, that he wished he had never written *Modern Chromatics.* He could never come to terms with the way his concepts had been applied by the artists of his day.

**Figure 2-11.**
Georges Seurat, *The Seine at Bourbevoic*, 1885. Oil on Canvas.
Seurat used the leading scientific theory of his day to develop his pointillist style of visual color mixing basing it on the writings of Chevreul and Rood. Look closely at the image and you can begin to see the dabs of color that make up the gradients. This style of painting is a very slow and methodical way of applying color.

### Albers, Itten, and the Bauhaus

Probably the most influential of all of the various groups on contemporary art and design was the Bauhaus. Johannes Itten and Joseph Albers (Itten's former student) taught at the school prior to its closing by the Nazis. Itten developed his color sphere and star, which was a flattened version of the sphere (Figure 2-12). Itten favored rectilinear design in a grid format because he believed that the most evident reaction of hues was at their edges where colors meet. These academic color studies were at the heart of the Bauhausian tradition. The shortcoming to all of the Bauhaus research was that it looked at color in a vacuum, as an independent element without any relation to imagery, function, or psychology.

Albers refined his teacher's work and continued these formal investigations of how colors interact with one another. He studied the optical illusions of color, making one color appear like two different colors, depending upon which color ground it was placed. He also found that two different hues could be made to look the same, depending upon which color ground they were placed. These were very formalistic color experiments usually done in simple geometric shapes such as squares and rectangles. In these studies, color was the key to the complete exclusion of imagery. He felt that throughout art history, color had been relegated to a minor role in place of imagery and abstraction. And as a result, during his tenure at Yale, Albers narrowed the scope of his work to very

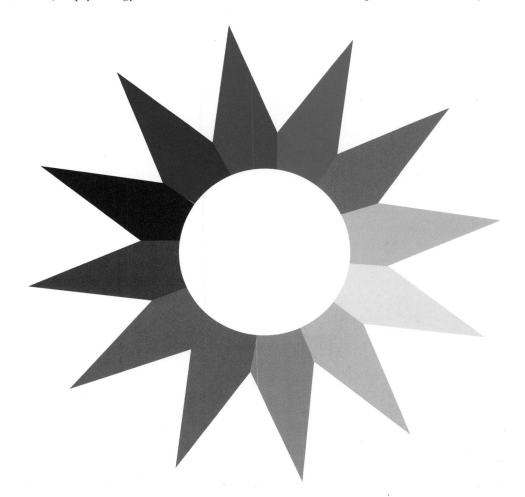

**Figure 2-12.**
An illustration of the twelve-hued Itten color star. The star is really a flattened-out sphere. Expanding out from the pure white center are tints of the various hues leading to the points of the star where the purest, most intense form of the hue is located.

**Figure 2-13.**
Joseph Albers, *Study for Homage to the Square: Beaming*, 1963.
© 2004 the Josef and Anni Albers Foundation/Artists Right Society ARS, New York. © Tate, London, 2003. Albers dedicated the latter part of his life to creating these studies. The format is always the same; only the hues change. The green center square seems to glow. This effect is heightened by isolating and surrounding it with lower-saturated shades of the same or a neighboring hue.

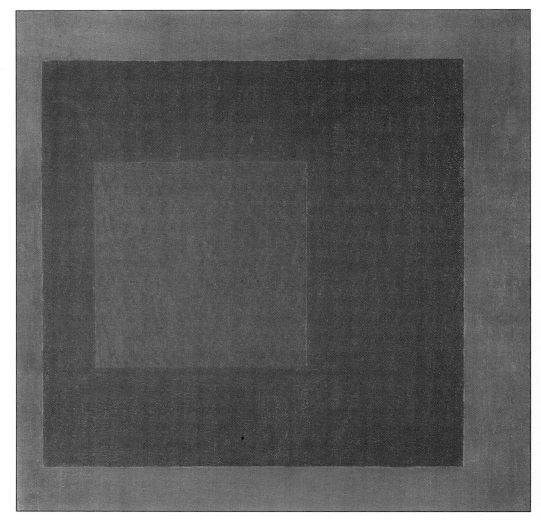

academic studies of the interactions of colors to one another. He began his Homage to the Square series exploring the full range of color interactions and relationships. In *Soft Light* (Figure 2-13), the radiance of the center square is created by the pale desaturated shades of the two outer squares. This creates a frame that intensifies the center square and makes it appear more luminous and brilliant. These works had a great deal of influence on the artists of the minimalist movement, many of whom were Albers's students at Yale. The minimalists were so-named because they sought to refine form to its most basic elements; they regularly worked with simple geometric shapes and forms. This group which included Carl Andre, Sol Lowit, and Donald Judd used very flat planes of highly saturated color in their work.

## Munsell

Albert H. Munsell might be considered the father of modern color classification. He was frustrated with the myriad of names for hues and the lack of ability to standardize color. Peach could be anything from a slight tint of red-orange to a strongly tinted hue of yellow-orange and anything in between. There were no formulas for mixing and matching colors. The same product produced in a plant in one state might not match the same product manufactured in another area of the country.

No standards for color naming, mixing, or classification existed.

Building on Rood's concept of color attributes, Munsell assigned a numerical notation system to these elements so that hues and their variations could be organized and classified. He developed a three-dimensional color wheel that placed value on the vertical axis (Figure 2-14). As you move up the central axis, the value moves from black at the bottom through the ranges of grays to white at the top. Ten hues were placed on the horizontal plane or spokes. Each spoke was a specific hue. The saturation for each hue went from dull gray at the center and moves to a pure, more saturated hue as they progress out from the center. This model allowed for a clear and objective approach to handing color with each step numbered along the way for easy classification.

Munsell's system starts to mark a departure from a purely theoretical approach to a more practical and technical approach. One of the keys to his system was to develop standards for manufacturing. The United States Bureau of Standards adopted his system as the appropriate language for working with color. While it is not as widely used today, it was the forerunner for our contemporary color matching systems such as Pantone, Toyo, and Trumatch.

## Commission International D'Eclairage (CIE)

In another effort to standardize color internationally, the Commission International D'Eclairage, or CIE, formed in 1931 and introduced their standardized color table. Their mission was to develop a precise color model for use in both scientific as well as artistic applications. This system would allow for accurate color matching using mathematical algorithms and mechanics, where previously color matching was based on subjective visual identification. As shown

**Figure 2-14.**
The Munsell 3-D Color Wheel. (Courtesy of GretagMacbeth). Munsell created a color 3-D solid, which allowed him to better express the relationship of a hue to its components of value and saturation. Value is represented along the center axis and saturation is expressed across each vertical spoke. The most saturated example of hue is shown at the outermost edge of each spoke.

**Figure 2-15.**
The CIE Color
Chromaticity Chart.
CIE Color Chart prepared
by LEDtronics, Inc.
(www.ledtronics.com).
The most intense hues
are located at the outer
edge of the upside-down
U-shaped diagram.
Colors are plotted along
an X,Y-axis in which
measurements are based
on light wavelengths and
not the actual hue.

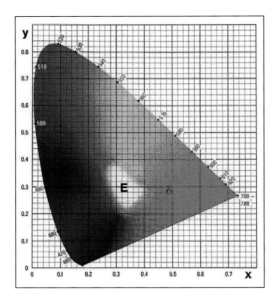

which measures hue, luminance (light
intensity), and saturation. These determine
the "chromaticity" of a color. This
information could then be quantified and
converted into statistical data and graphed.
The upside-down U-shaped CIE chromaticity
diagram shown in Figure 2-15 shows all of
the spectral hues with cyan and green having
the largest range. The warmer hues take up
a much smaller area at the bottom and the
"E" in the center stands for "equal energy"
or the neutral addition of all of the hues.

The CIE LAB color model was developed
for the growing computer industry and it is a
device-independent color system. This means
that its color values are described according to
normal viewing conditions, therefore allowing
it to act as a universal translator. The "L" (in
LAB) stands for luminance while the "A" and
"B" channels hold the color information. This
permits a user to adjust the sharpness or details
in a given image without changing the color.

in Figure 2-15, the CIE devised its color
concept based on the additive process using
the primaries: red, green, and blue (RGB).
These values also related to the short,
medium, and long wavelengths of the cones,
or color receptors, found in the human eye.
Subsequent models included the CIE LAB
model, which became significant to the
creation and application of digital color
systems. The additive process differentiated
the CIE model from all of the other systems
discussed so far, which had been based on
subtractive color.

The CIE is a technical, scientific, and
cultural nonprofit organization. Membership
is purely voluntary; however, the benefit of
being a member is to have and create color
models or systems that are not proprietary
and can be used all over the world. In a
sense, they could be considered the "United
Nations" of light and color. The organization
is divided into several major groups covering
such diverse areas as Vision and Color, the
Measurement of Light and Radiation,
Interior Environment and Lighting Design,
Photobiology and Photochemistry, and
Computer Image Technology.

The initial exact color matching was
achieved using a device called a **colorimeter**,

### International Color Consortium (ICC) and Inter-Society Color Council (ISCC)

The work of the International Color
Consortium (ICC) and the Inter-Society
Color Council (ISCC) dovetails with the
mission of the CIE. But these two organizations are primarily concerned with digital
color and color consistency. Adobe was one
of the founding members of the ICC along
with seven other computer companies whose
mission was to standardize color across
several different platforms. Their intent
was to translate color data created on one
device into another device's native color
space. This would enable users to move
easily from one piece of equipment to
another: from scanner to computer and
computer to printer and so on. It allowed
tremendous flexibility for both users and
vendors to translate the imbedded color
profiles between different software packages
and operating platforms. This added to the

ease of use and, without it, the personal computer as an art and design tool would never have flourished.

## Digital Color

In the late 1980s, computer technology began to proliferate and signaled the arrival of what could be called the era of the personal computer. The PC, or personal computer, made computing and digital applications available and accessible to a nontechnical public. These developments led to the mass marketing of computer technology for the home and office. The door was opened for a new theory of color to emerge: digital color theory. But theory was bypassed in favor of technology. As Adobe and other software companies began developing imaging and illustration software, color modes and devices to select color were created as part of the new packages. For example, the Adobe color picker was not based on any previous color theory.

The color space was created to be device dependent and to relate to the monitors and printers required to display the work created. When you look at the color space on the Adobe color picker (Figure 2-16), you see a slice of a three-dimensional cube. It is set up on an X,Y,Z-axis. As you move along any of the three color spaces available—HVS, RGB, or LAB—each letter and its corresponding selection button allows the user to view a thin shaving of the cube and thereby make a color selection comprising the hue, its value, and saturation in one mouse-click. Theory is no longer the driving force. The underlying mathematical algorithm is computer generated. In the past, the user would have been required to generate or write all of the underlying code in some software language; now it is completely transparent. The user makes a selection from the toolbar or menu and in a single mouse-click, the color is selected and applied.

## Nadin

Mihai Nadin, a major voice in contemporary computational philosophy, writes in his new book *Anticipation—The End Is Where We Start From* that everything we are currently doing or are engaged in is in anticipation of what we will do next. In other words, we are always living in a future tense. In this mode of thinking, we see color because we expect to see color. Grass is green because we expect it to be green. Even color-blind people will perceive and, in essence, see grass as green because of their cultural conditioning and education. But this aspect of color deficiency reinforces the fact that color information is processed in two distinct ways. First, the information received through the eyes is processed by the brain, which is primarily a physiological function. Second, there is the personal contribution, previous experiences, cultural upbringing, and other interactions. All of these factors lead us to make color predictions in what we see and expect to see.

Even the unexpected encounter, the nonanticipated event, is still primarily a function of the mind and only in small part due to the place or event itself. People regularly construct false anticipations and live by them. When one of these predictions

**Figure 2-16.**
The Adobe color picker is based on a solid color cube. Each color space represents a slice of the cube. The top right corner is the most pure saturated version of the hue. Moving along the top of the cube gives the user tints, down the right side shades, the far left side of the cube is a gray scale, and the balance of the area are tones of that hue. (Courtesy of Adobe Systems, Inc.)

**Figure 2-17.**
*The Wizard of Oz,*
The Emerald City. 1939.
(Courtesy of MGM.)
Many films move from
black and white to color
to show either a dream
sequence or a fantasy
segment. In many of
these films, reality is
shown as black and
white. How many other
films can you name that
use this same technique?

fail, the person simply includes the new data reconstructing the expectation, a concept that is akin to the psychological theory of cognitive dissonance.

## Chromophobia

David Batchelor, one of the pioneers of contemporary color theory, coined the term **chromophobia,** which is also the title of his recent book. Chromophobia is the fear of color and of the use of color. Batchelor looked at popular culture and film, as well as digital technology. He wrote that black and white were masculine, while color was feminine. He looked at films that used both black and white and color to tell their stories. One such example, *The Wizard of Oz*, starts off with Dorothy living in a gray world, Kansas. To experience color, she must leave home and travel to the land of Oz (Figure 2-17). It is only here in the dream or fantasy world that color exists, full Technicolor, radiant and bright. But in the end she must leave the world

of color and return to gray: family and home, and the boring sameness of daily life on the plains. Other films, such as *Pleasantville, Memento,* and *Wings of Desire,* use this motif as a way of creating a counterpoint between reality and fantasy or a dream state. Reality is always shown in black and white as if it is missing something, while the fantasy or dream world is in vivid color.

More importantly, Batchelor also speaks about the difference between color in the tube and the can. Starting in the 1950s and into the 1960s, artists abandoned the traditional tube of paint and turned to the hardware store and premixed cans of house paint. It is the hand versus the machine or "ready-made." Throughout the history of art, the artist was connected to the palette—the place where color was mixed by the artist's hand and applied to the canvas. There was a direct relationship between the palette and color mixing, color mixing to traditional color theory, and color theory to the color circle. And the circle has dominated color theory from Newton to Munsell. But with the move to the can, artists moved from the circle to the color chart. The color chart (Figure 2-18) is nothing more than a simple list in which every color is equivalent to every other color and independent of every other color. No great hierarchies exist, only random selections of color. The color circle is analogical and the color chart is

digital; therefore, it refers directly to contemporary modernity.

With current printing technology, digital color is apt to be flat, shiny, and intense. The intensity of digital color tends to localize it unlike the broad generalized color created on the artist's palette. Muted colors that are considered more tasteful appeal to those in a higher socioeconomic bracket, while bright saturated hues may be considered more common, popularist, and egalitarian. The

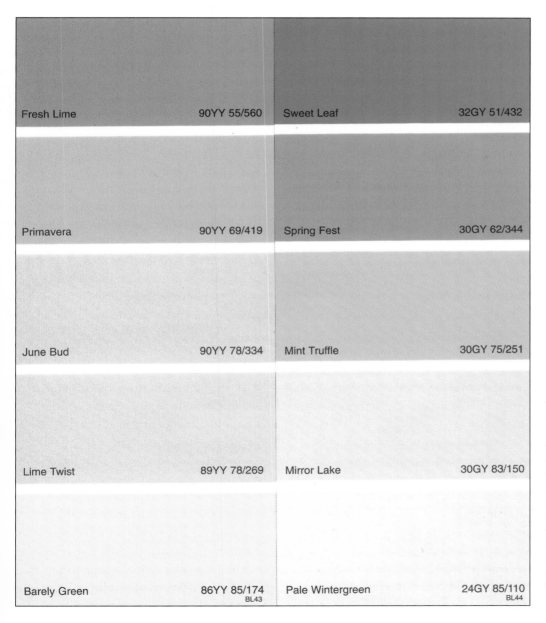

| | | |
|---|---|---|
| Fresh Lime | 90YY 55/560 | Sweet Leaf    32GY 51/432 |
| Primavera | 90YY 69/419 | Spring Fest    30GY 62/344 |
| June Bud | 90YY 78/334 | Mint Truffle    30GY 75/251 |
| Lime Twist | 89YY 78/269 | Mirror Lake    30GY 83/150 |
| Barely Green | 86YY 85/174  BL43 | Pale Wintergreen    24GY 85/110  BL44 |

**Figure 2-18.** Glidden Paint color swatches. Glidden, an ICI Paints brand. Batchelor believes color swatches represent a break from the traditional color wheel and are more representative of contemporary color philosophy. The artist no longer mixes colors on a palette, but selects color from premixed swatches. These color swatches also have a direct relationship to the way colors can be selected on a computer.

computer, especially the personal computer, democratized color. In addition, these flat saturated hues keep the viewer at a distance, giving off a more industrial or mechanical look to the work.

Digital color is not only visually flat, it also lacks any true physical texture. The tactility of traditional paint mixed on a palette and applied by a brush is gone. Virtually all printers (laser or inkjet) lay down a thin microlayer of colored ink or pigment. This creates a smooth texture-free surface. Texture, or more correctly, the simulation of texture, can be created only within the virtual confines of the software package or computer. For example, in the latest version of Photoshop, the new "brushes palette" now has a texture mode or option. The user can decide on an array of simulated textures, such as canvas. Otherwise, texture is absent in today's technology and gone with it is the "hand" of the artist, or so some would say. This has become one of the great debates raging at art conferences and gatherings all over the world.

**Color Forecasting**

Color forecasting is another form of color theorizing, although it is not intended for classification and categorization. It is for purely aesthetic use by designers and artists. The Color Association United States (CAUS) may be one of the oldest color-forecasting services. Others include the Color Council and Trend Union. These color-forecasting services began when manufacturers and designers cut off by World War I could not get dyes, fabrics, fashion style directions, and other information from Europe. Since then, they have become industry staples in fashion, interior, industrial, product, and graphic design. The services work in a similar manner. A group of experts from both the design and manufacturing areas meet to

discuss all aspects of product sales and development. Based on these factors, color forecasters make predictions or develop themes for the coming seasons. They may develop specific palettes for different industries or economic groups. These palettes represent trends that may come into the market in the next eighteen to twenty-four months. Color-forecasting services always make their predictions several seasons in advance to allow for manufacturing time, and, therefore, designers are always working well ahead of what is happening in the current market.

Forecasting services and associations allow designers to have an understanding of the future direction of color, including trends from movies, music, as well as the development of new colors and buying trends. If these were not available, designers would have to either do all of the market research on their own or make guesses, which could be very costly if the choices turned out to be poor ones. Few students realize that while in school they may be able to choose their favorite colors for their design projects, but that in the professional world, colors are selected through intensive market research. Color-forecasting services give the designer up-to-date information in these areas.

Ellen Lynch-Goldstein, designer and Chair of the Accessories Design Department at the Fashion Institute of Technology, explains how designers use color forecasting in the fashion industries. "The industry uses color-forecasting services as a barometer to see what's predicted and to develop their own ideas. Forecasts that are primarily international are not as important to the American market as they are to Europe. For example, if a forecast predicts that yellow will be a hot color in accessories, American designers will incorporate that color into other colors to give just a hint of yellow, while the European market will use full yellow bags (Figure 2-19) and shoes as a 'basic' color."

This is a good explanation of how the designers view these services. The forecasts are used as guides and not strictly adhered to. They give the design community an idea of the directions color may take in the coming seasons.

## Summary

All of the myriad of theories that have been developed have one thing in common: they all try to make sense out of what is arguably the most complex of all of the design elements— color. All artists and designers have been influenced by this work. Each theorist built on his predecessor's work, either incorporating it into his own work or in the case of Goethe, outright rejecting Newton's ideas. Some, like Seurat, based their entire life's work on the theory of one person or another. These theories gave us the concepts of the primary and secondary hues and tried to place them in some sort of context.

As technology and manufacturing became more prevalent, the theories shifted to developing a common language or method for the application of color. Contemporary theorists such as Batchelor and others are trying to make sense of new mediums and their relationship to color. As new strides in technology create new applications, so too will contemporary theories be developed and presented to help us make sense of these new color spaces and to use them to their fullest.

**Figure 2-19.**
Joanne O'Reilly, *Handmade Purse*, 2004.
Digitally created image on fabric, hand-stitched with embellished appliqué.
Fashion-forecasting services predicted that bright hues, including yellow, would be a dominant color in fashion. O'Reilly says that pet themes have been projected as up-and-coming imagery for clothing and accessories this year. The playful fish motif on this handbag fits nicely into this schema. O'Reilly feels that designers must stay on top of new trends and that forecasting services play an essential role in planning her upcoming lines.

**3**

## Color Psychology: Chapter 3

Have you ever felt blue? We use color in our language on a regular basis to describe feelings and emotions. People are said to be "green with envy," "in the pink," or "seeing red." They can be "true blue," "white as a ghost," or a "yellow-bellied coward." Even our medals for bravery and heroism have a color: the Purple Heart honors the wounded in combat.

Color and emotions are so closely related that we use these terms as descriptions for concepts and feelings that go beyond words and language.

Color plays a vital role in culture and daily life and may be the single most important aspect of a painting, product, or design. It is not enough for an artist or designer to produce a particular product in any color of their choosing: they must be aware of how their choice will affect the viewer. In design, the simple act of choosing a color can make or break a product. Even a vast knowledge of color harmonies, such as how two or more hues may be mixed to create an infinite number of new hues, will not ensure that viewers derive the artist's intended message.

**Figure 3-1.**
Gentile Da Fabriano, *The Adoration of the Magi,* 1423.
The Virgin Mary's robes of deep blue evolved into navy blue, with all of the associations of virtue, truth, and honesty.

Why do people favor one color over another and what does it all really mean?

When we look at anything from a painting to a package or even a simple product, we bring a lifetime's worth of memories, experiences, and psychological baggage that impacts and affects our perception. Color psychology and market research go hand in hand, but these two areas have had an uneasy relationship or alliance since the days of Sigmund Freud. Psychologists and psychiatric professionals are concerned with pure academic scholarship and the need to understand and make sense of the psyche. Their research may result in new diagnostic tools and therapies, as well as a better understanding of the human mind. Market research, on the other hand, might be considered the application of this knowledge for commerce and industry.

Whichever your primary focus, the goal is understanding this complex relationship of color, psyche, and emotion that enables artists and designers to produce effective works of art and designs. The artist must have more than the technical knowledge of creating and mixing color, but must also understand its impact on the viewer. This knowledge enables the artist and designer to intentionally create a work that will elicit the specific desired response from the viewer.

### A History of Blue

Color associations can change and be as relative as the application of color itself. Blue can stand for being "true blue," loyal, and steadfast. These identifications with the hue go as far back as 1340 B.C. to the Egyptian civilization and the reign of King Tut. In western culture, the color blue dates to 431 A.D. when the church began to associate specific colors with the saints and religious figures to bring the stories of the Bible to life. The gem, lapis lazuli (a deep blue), was

ground into pigment and used to paint the clothing of the Virgin Mary. It quickly became associated with her traits of piety, truth, and goodness (Figure 3-1). The contemporary, mass-produced equivalent is navy blue, which is still associated with truth, honesty, and confidence. Certainly no businessman or politician would be without a navy suit! Blue is America's favorite color, reminding us of peaceful, easy times. Denim reminds us of jeans and invokes the era of the cowboy and the West. It is the color of calm associated with water and sky, and the earth is even referred to as a "big blue marble."

### Picasso's Blue Period

The very same hue that is associated with peace, virtue, and truth, is also the color we use to describe someone who is depressed and sullen. There are wonderful anecdotal stories that Pablo Picasso used this color predominately, in what is now referred to as his "Blue Period," because he was very poor and could only afford blue paint. While these stories make great copy, and have become part of the Picasso legend, we know that this period in his work starts with the death by suicide of his closest friend, Casagemas.

**Figure 3-2**
Pablo Picasso, *La Mort de Casagemas*, 1901.
© 2004 Estate of Pablo Picasso/Artists Rights Society (ARS), New York.
The color palette used contains warm hues and gives the viewer the feeling that the person lying in the coffin has only recently passed away. The candle is a visual metaphor for life—when the candle is extinguished, so is life. It might be Picasso's way of holding on to his friend's memory.

**Figure 3-3.**
Pablo Picasso,
*Casagemas in His
Coffin,* 1901.
© 2004 Estate of
Pablo Picasso/Artists
Rights Society (ARS),
New York.
Now the colors are blue
and cold. The colors give
us a feeling of emptiness
and complete stillness.
The cool palette also
helps distance us from
the figure.

(Figure 3-3), which shows his friend cold and dead, lying in his casket. The features are gaunt and the color is completely desaturated. The flame of the candle, a metaphor for life, in the previous work has long been extinguished and is absent in this picture. In this later painting, Picasso used blue because it summed up his mood and conveyed to the viewer his sense of emptiness and sorrow. This is the power of color.

**Psychological Perception**

Beyond a poetic use of hue and pigment, as we have seen in the previous chapter, colors have a physiological effect on our bodies and well-being. The color red will increase skin temperature and raise blood pressure and respiration, while blue will lower skin temperature, blood pressure, respiration, and pulse. Mink ranchers use blue lights to keep the normally vicious and ill-tempered animals calm and to allow them to handle the animals more easily. Color can also affect our perception of objects as well. On the English waterfront, dock workers complained that a product packed in very dark pigmented containers was too heavy and a strike nearly ensued. The shippers replaced the dark containers with containers colored a soft-tinted hue. The new "lighter" boxes pleased the dock workers and talk of a strike passed without issue. The size and weight of the boxes remained the same; only the color changed and with it the perception of their heft and manageability.

**Mood and Emotion**

Mood and disposition can also influence our perception of color. As an experiment on color and emotion, the U.S. Navy painted its holding cells in the "brig," its military jail, pink. They found that even the most hostile and agitated sailors became docile and calm while in the pink holding area. Why did this happen? One might

The death of his best friend started a serious bout of depression that lasted several years. It just so happens that these years correspond to the Blue Period, a time in which Picasso primarily uses the color blue in all of his paintings. Picasso created several paintings of his friend lying in state. In one of the first paintings, *La Mort de Casagemas,* the hues used are bright and hot and give a warm glow to the figure (Figure 3-2). We see the backlit head of Casagemas, and the yellow highlights in the face, which still has the soft warmth of life. Only the mark of the gunshot wound belies the fact that he is dead and not sleeping.

Juxtaposed to this is what might be considered the first of the Blue Period paintings, *Casagemas in His Coffin*

**Figure 3-4.**
People adjust better
to new surroundings
in a green room. The
bed-and-breakfast inn
uses this underlying
psychology in its choice
of colors for its rooms
to make their guests
feel welcome and
more at home.

think that it would have just the opposite effect. The color pink was emasculating and made the prisoners feel withdrawn and less manly and made them easier to control. However, the study also revealed that if the prisoners were left in the pink holding cell for more than a short period of time, they become even more aggressive and violent. The color that at first subdued and quieted, over an extended period of time, irritated and aggravated the sailors so much that they became uncontrollable.

While pink may be questionable to use in certain situations, green, on the other hand can be a very welcoming hue. People adjust well to new surroundings under the influence of green (Figure 3-4). If you paint the interior of a cabin at a sleep-away camp green, there will be fewer incidences of homesickness among the children. Green interiors are also frequently used in bed-and-breakfast inns to create a warm and inviting atmosphere for the guests.

## Color and Appetite

While the U.S. Navy's experiments with color may have failed, fast-food restaurant chains have perfected the use of color to sway emotion. Think about your favorite: McDonald's, Burger King, or Wendy's. All use the same basic color scheme of hot hues of yellow, orange, and red. These colors increase the appetite. Not only do you order and eat more under the influence of these hues, you eat faster. The idea is to get you in, stimulate your appetite, and get you out of there as fast as possible so that the next customer can come in and take your place. The brightly colored, hard plastic seats in these establishments are not just for sanitation and easy cleaning, but are to keep you from getting too comfortable and lingering. Time is money. On the other hand, upscale restaurants use soft lighting, and dark subdued hues of greens, blues, and violets. They want you to relax, to take your time and linger over another after-dinner drink. Here, more time means more money, a higher bill, and more profit to the proprietor.

## Color and Flavor

In food stores, bread is normally sold in packaging decorated or tinted with golden

**Figure 3-5.**
A blue soft drink. All of the new blue foods on the market have a bright intense color. For soda and sports drinks, the color reminds the consumer of something cold and refreshing. What flavor do you think the drink is?

and can help to reduce the amount of food you consume. The "blue plate special" made famous in the 1930s used this same concept. The color of the plate affects the look of the food and thereby causes the patron to eat less and feel full faster—another dieting tip.

If you still have any reservations that color affects flavor, take a look at the ingredients on most food products and you will see that one or more of the items listed is a coloring agent or dye. Without the addition of caramel color, Coke would not be a rich brown, but would be a clear colorless liquid such as Seven Up. The color pink will enhance the taste of sweetness in any food product. This is one reason why many bakeries use pink boxes for their cakes and cookies. When we see bright purple edibles or drinks, we expect them to taste like grapes and so on.

The most recent entry into the food-coloring fray is blue (Figure 3-5). In the past, blue was not considered edible because it was not a color found in fresh, natural food products; rather, it reminded customers of mold and decay. Even today, the blue that is used is a very saturated bright hue and never a blue green. These new products are mostly directed to a younger market who have not yet formed negative color associations and usually it is used in candy, soft drinks, and sports drinks.

or brown tones to promote the idea of home-baked oven freshness. Rarely will you see it sold in a green wrapper because the color cast onto the product would remind buyers of mold. Adding yellow to the wrapper will boost bread sales and give the product a sunny bright appeal. When margarine first was introduced, there were laws in the dairy states preventing manufacturers from coloring the product yellow, the color of butter. Initially it came with a separate packet of yellow dye; the consumer would have to mix it in to make the white, pasty substance resemble the natural product.

In fact if you are on a diet, replace the normal light bulb in your refrigerator with a blue bulb. The food will look unappetizing

## Socioeconomic Aspects of Color

Your color choices are determined by many factors. There are socioeconomic aspects that affect your choice of favorite hues and that determine which hues you feel more at home or comfortable with. The higher your economic status, the more you will favor darker, less saturated, complex hues. People in the lower economic brackets tend to prefer and respond favorably to simple, bright, pure hues. This can been seen in everything from department stores to hotels. For instance,

Target, a discount department store, uses bright red, while Tiffany's, an ultra high-end retailer, is known for their use of a muted turquoise palette. This color has become so synonymous with Tiffany's that people only have to see the soft blue box to know where the item was purchased. Socioeconomic factors influence everything, including the choice of color for your car, says Carlton Wagner, a color consultant. Someone buying a Ford may be comfortable choosing brown, while another person in a higher economic bracket who is buying a Lexus will not respond well to brown. Instead, this person will choose sable, a deeper more complex shade of the same color. The one group that Wagner says does not fit this model is the so-called yuppie (young urban professional). Yuppies tend to pick color choices based on where they want to go, and they look ahead to the next higher economic bracket for their color choices.

### Oppenheim's Blue Shirt

Further indication that colors have socioeconomic connotations is evidenced in how we relate color to the names given to certain occupations. "White-collar" workers are executives and others engaged in office work. "Blue-collar" denotes manual labor and has undertones of negative associations of the working class as unskilled and undereducated. Such was the controversy that swarmed when Milwaukee's General Mitchell Airport announced plans to erect a new work of art, Dennis Oppenheim's *Blue Shirt* (Figure 3-6). When the piece was first unveiled to the public, it was felt that it was derogatory and a slap in the face to the city's working class. But the artist felt that the piece was positive and exalted the working class that is the core of the city. He also felt that the piece dealt with the human anatomy and how inherited traits and the choices we make through our purchases become a part

of our personalities. Here the color and item fused together to imbue the image with many meanings, opening it up to vast interpretations. Only time will tell if this work becomes synonymous with Milwaukee as the St. Louis Arch and the Washington Monument have to their respective locales.

### Learned Color Responses

Our response to color is not purely unconscious or intuitive; it is learned. Blue for boys and pink for girls is a cultural response to color taught to us by our family and reinforced in the marketplace. Colors are

**Figure 3-6.**
Dennis Oppenheim, *Blue Shirt*, 2003. Proposal for the General Mitchell International Airport, Milwaukee, Wisconsin. Courtesy of Dennis Oppenheim. There was protest against the work because many people thought Oppenheim was making fun of the blue-collar workers, which he was not. He felt the piece was a monument to their work ethic.

**Figure 3-7.**
Bumblebee.
The yellow and black stripes of a bumblebee signal danger. Even if you did not know that bees could sting, you would still be wary of any thing or animal with these colors or markings.

**Figure 3-8.**
Green stop sign. Would you stop at a green stop sign?

fire trucks and hydrants because it can be seen from farthest away, regardless of the light and time of day. Years from now when schoolchildren are asked what color fire trucks are, they will answer "yellow-green."

Another learned response to color is our reaction to the combination of yellow and black (Figure 3-7). They are the colors of poison and danger. Bumblebees, wasps, police caution tape, and road hazard warning signs all contain these two colors. So, while they are easy to recognize and read, they are not inviting and rarely used in design.

**Color Function and Cognition**

By changing the color of an object, we can drastically alter its function and use. We tend to recognize objects such as signs by their color as much as by their shape or lettering. Red is the color of a stop sign and whether it is the octagonal shape as in America or a circular format as in Europe, the color red automatically signals us to stop. What would happen if you painted the sign green? Would

also cultural and have religious connotations. For example, in India black is used for weddings and white is used for funerals— the direct opposite of our western view. For years, fire trucks have been painted red, hence the name "fire-engine red." But several years ago it was discovered that this red hue is hard to see at dawn and dusk when there is little light. Today, yellow-green is used for

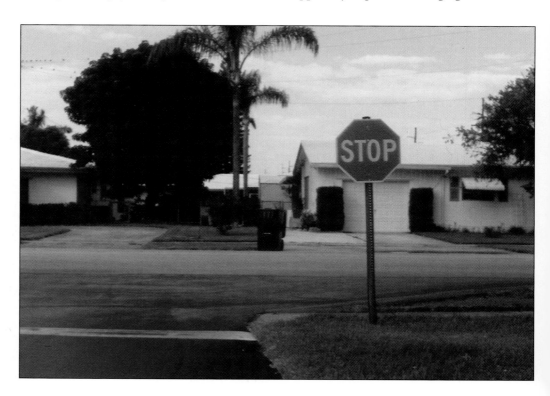

people stop? In several psychological studies over the years in controlled situations, stop signs were changed from red to green (Figure 3-8). Everything else about the signs remained exactly the same. Drivers would regularly go right through the intersections without stopping. When pulled over by the researchers, the people in the car would say, "Yes, I saw the stop sign." When asked why they failed to come to a complete stop, their answer invariably was "But the sign was green and green means go." The drivers were more influenced by the color of the sign than the printed word or the shape of the sign.

What other objects can you think of that are always a specific color and never vary?

## Packaging and Products

The exact opposite of this approach would be the way food and beverages are packaged. Here color is used to signify the object as well as to enhance the flavor or taste. We recognize specific brands of food, cigarettes, and even magazines by their trademark colors. We reach for a product by recognizing the color of the package before we have even consciously read the name of the product. Shoppers scan the shelf and recognize the product they wish to purchase in 0.03 seconds. We recognize the color yellow of the Cheerios box (Figure 3-9) long before we see or read the name of the product.

What other products do you recognize solely by their color?

In market research studies it has been determined that 60 percent of acceptance or rejection of a product is based on its color. That decision is also made very quickly. Within 90 seconds, a person will make a choice to accept or reject a purchase. Any discussions after that initial time period will rarely change the person's mind but will be used to reinforce the decision for or against.

But by far the most important aspect is the color of the item. If the color is not right, people will not purchase the product.

If you don't think the color of an item is this critical, consider the role it plays in the purchase of a major ticket item such as a car. You go to the dealership and order your dream car including all of the options and extras and wait for it to arrive from the factory. A few weeks pass and the salesman from the dealership calls and says the car is in, but there is just one small problem—there was a minor mix up and the color is slightly different. Instead of the deep intense red you ordered, it is bright orange with pink stripes.

**Figure 3-9.**
A box of Cheerios. We see the color yellow before we read the label. We quickly learn to associate the color of the package to our favorite products and reach for them based on recognizing the specific hue as we shop.

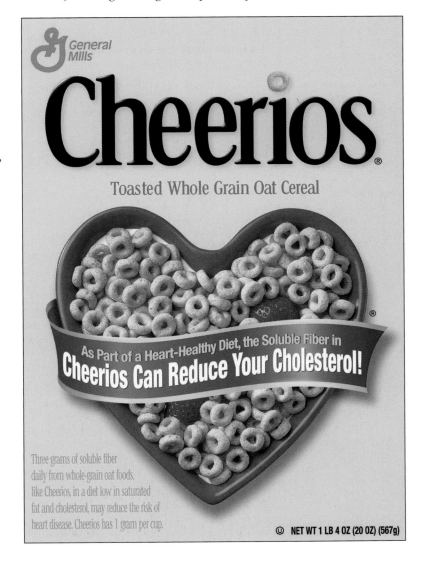

Orange and pink are close to red, the color you ordered. Would it make a difference to you? Of course it would.

Color is important. The choice of color will have many determining factors such as age, sex, and socioeconomic class of the intended customer. Colors that work for one group of buyers may not work for another, and colors that may be acceptable for one product may not be appropriate for another.

### Apple Changes Everything

One of the newest products to be sold in a variety of colors is the computer. Traditionally, they came in the standard gray or putty color. They had an institutional generic look without any thought to the color or style. The one exception to this was the laptop computer, which was generally a dark gray tone. The reason for this was that consumer research studies showed that the public felt the dark gray color was richer, more business-like, and more astute. Consumers also thought that dark gray gave the product a more compact look. Then, in the late 1990s, Apple came along with the iBook and iMac and revolutionized the world of home computers.

Today, the computer is a fashion accessory and decorative home item. It is now considered a part of the room like furniture, and color is used to accent and decorate it. Other companies such as Dell have followed Apple's lead in creating colorful home computers. This same styling is also being featured in other items, from the George Foreman grill to microwave ovens and a whole host of other products.

**Figure 3-10.**
Albert Bierstadt, *In the Mountains*, 1867. Wadsworth Atheneum, Hartford. Gift of John J. Morgan in memory of his mother, Juliet Pierpont Morgan. Bierstadt's painting is a good example of atmospheric perspective. Notice how the color in the foreground is light and bright, while the background is gray and desaturated. As things blend into the background, they also lose detail and become hazy.

## Artists' Use of Color

It is not only the hue that is important in our perception of color; saturation and brightness are also essential elements. Warm, bright, fully saturated colors appear to advance—they make objects seem larger and closer to us. Intense and highly saturated hues are normally used in the foreground and bring the viewer into the painting or work of art. Tints will also create a similar optical boost and open up the space, which makes objects appear larger and closer to the viewer. These will also imbue the image with a positive, uplifting feeling.

On the other hand, cool, dull, low saturated dark colors make objects look smaller and appear to recede in space. They have a restrained feeling and evoke emotions such as sadness, depression, loss, and longing. As objects move back into space, they lose color and saturation and blend or melt away into a middle or light gray. This effect is called **atmospheric perspective** (Figure 3-10). As items move into the background, there is less light falling on them and subsequently there is less color, detail, and texture. This is why when we look at a mountain range, for instance, the peaks seem to dissolve into thin air and fade away. It is a more realistic and natural way of using color to enhance depth and distance.

When working in a representational manner with color, it is referred to as working with **local color**. Local color and value are synonymous with the exact appearance of the object. In Pat Rosenstein's painting, *The Ack Bassward Painting*, the colors used accurately reflect the natural colors of the objects portrayed (Figure 3-11). This style of painting is also known as photorealism. This use of color to mimic objects and their surroundings can act as a type of camouflage and is also known as **trompe l'oeil**, which means "to fool the eye."

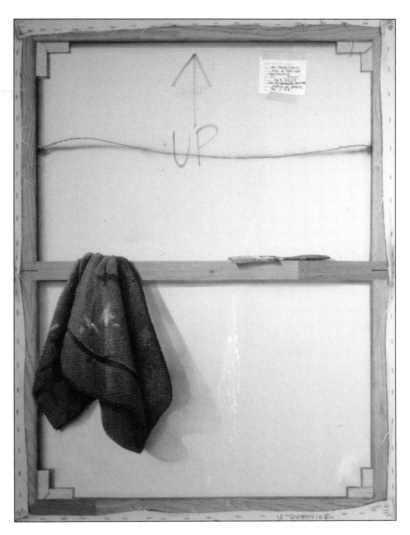

## Color As a Means of Expression

Another method of using color as visual expression is the use of **heightened color**. Heightened color makes elements of a painting or image stand out. In France, the Fauves (or "wild beasts," as the name translates) used this theory of color to make their images stand out (Figure 3-12). This was also a liberating idea that an artist could paint an object—for instance, a tree—any color he wanted. And by making the tree blue or red or violet, force the viewer to stop and rethink just exactly what a tree is and what its true meaning may be. Further, it gave the object a power and intensity it would not normally have. Color could be used for color's sake

**Figure 3-11.**
Pat Rosenstein, *The Ack Bassward Painting*, 1998. At first glance, this looks like a photograph of the back of a canvas. Rosenstein captures the local colors accurately and correctly in this photorealistic work. The shadow of the wire running across the back of the canvas appears to be protruding out into space while in reality, it is flat.

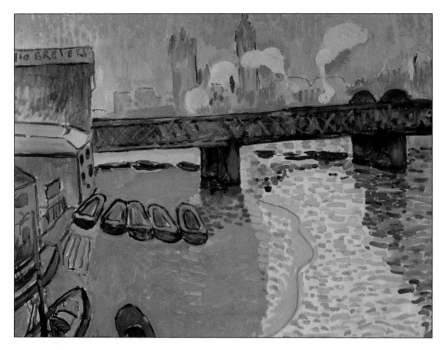

**Figure 3-12.**
Andre Derain, *Charing Cross Bridge*, 1906. © 2004 Artists Rights Society (ARS), New York/ADAGP, Paris Derain used a heightened or arbitrary color palette to convey emotion and was not concerned with the natural or local color of the items. He used colors for their dramatic impact. This might also be considered the first steps into abstraction.

alone without any relation to the natural world. To the artists of the early 1900s, this was a powerful liberating force.

Prior to this, all art had to relate back to the natural world in both color and form. Even the Impressionists, as radically new as they were for their time, still maintained this naturalistic link—a tree trunk was brown, the sky various shades of blue, and so on. The Fauves made a distinct break with the past and all forms of naturalism and realism, and their work foreshadowed the advent of abstraction.

Outlasting the Fauves during this time period were the German artists of The Bridge (Die Brucke) and the Blue Rider (Der Blaue Reiter), more commonly known as German Expressionists. They used identical concepts of enhanced and elevated color to imbue their paintings with strong emotional and psychological content. Artists began to understand the power that color alone could achieve in pushing the cerebral and expressive state of an artwork. This idea of the use of heightened color reemerged in the 1980s in the work of the neo-Expressionists such as Sandro Chia, Jean-Michel Basquiat,

and others. They were reacting in opposition to what they saw as the overly intellectualized work of minimalism and conceptual art. Just as with their earlier counterparts, they sought to bring an emotional and visceral feeling to the artwork they created. In *Untitled (Skull),* Basquiat uses very fluid gestural brush strokes to convey the feeling of quick rapid movement (Figure 3-13). The hurried strokes have the feel of graffiti that is accentuated by the quasi-written scrawl in the top left and bottom right of the picture. The warm hues reinforce the action and create a frenetic underlying rhythm to the work. The gaze of the skull is vague and unfixed, adding to the unsettling feel of the work.

**Color and Psychoanalysis**

Psychiatrists have long been interested in perception and color and their combined effect on the psyche. While Sigmund Freud was one of the first to begin to discuss the use of color and its relationship to psychology in his monograph on Leonardo da Vinci, it was Carl Jung in *Man and His Symbols* who began to see color as a primal

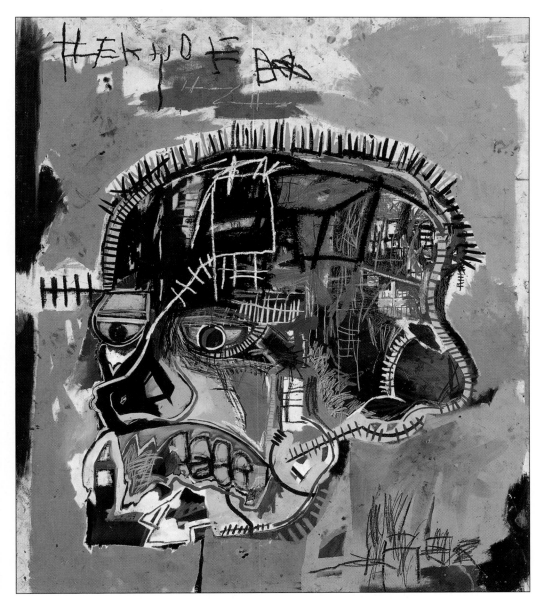

**Figure 3-13.**
Jean-Michel Basquiat, *Untitled (Skull)*, 1981. © 2004 Artists Rights Society (ARS), New York/ADAGP, Paris. The warm bright hues in the skull create a feeling of frenetic movement and push the image to the foreground. As the colors move into the background, they become less saturated, which helps to create a sense of depth. As with earlier expressionist movements, color is used for its emotional content without regard for the natural world.

element that needed to be addressed. He saw the artist's use of color as a manifestation of the unconscious. Laurie Schneider Adams sees a close relationship between art and psychology, and she believes that the artist's use of the color, form, and imagery are autobiographical in nature.

## The Luscher Color Test

In 1960, Dr. Max Luscher developed a color test to determine personality traits and disorders. The Luscher Color Test has become the standard and is considered the most reliable of all of the color personality insight tools because it held its results even for those with color vision impairment or color blindness. The simple and most widely used version of the test contains eight colors. The four psychological primaries—dark blue, yellow, red-orange, and green—make up the first group of the color test, with violet and neutrals of brown, gray, and black (the absence of all color) making up the second or auxiliary group. These auxiliary colors

**Figure 3-14.**
An illustration of the eight color swatches that make up the Luscher Color Test. Pick your favorite color from among the samples and then match your choice to the corresponding explanation. How accurately does the statement reflect your personality?

require a bit of an explanation: black and gray are not actually colors at all because they represent the negation of all color. Violet is a mixture of dark blue and red-orange, while brown is actually a mixture of red-orange and black. By placing these colored swatches in descending order of preference, it revealed aspects of personality, including anxieties, conflicts, and compulsions.

Look at the eight color swatches in Figure 3-14 and choose the one you like the most. Don't think about what your favorite color is, but rather which one of these particular patches you prefer. In the full color test, you would then rate each of the eight swatches in order from most to least favorite. Position one is the color you most prefer and represents what you want most or covet. It is your greatest desire. The color picked in position eight is the least preferred and represents what you seek to avoid. This order would give insight into your personality and psyche. The number of possible combinations that are detailed in Luscher's book gives a more complete picture of the subject's personality. Look in the following and find your first choice. How well does it match up to your personality?

**Dark blue** represents total calm, tranquility, harmony, and comfort, and relates to one's need for contentment and

fulfillment. When picked in the first position, it represents a need for emotional stability, for rest, relaxation, and the desire to re-charge. The person choosing blue wants a calm and orderly environment. If it is a person's first choice, it is usually chosen for itself and not as a rejection of another color.

**Blue-green** used in the test contains a small amount of blue. It is an expression of steadfastness—standing up tall and firm like a tree. People who choose green in the first position can be assertive and demanding, primarily concerned with themselves and their personal gains. It could be called the "me" color of people who want to add to their own personal fortune. It is no accident that this is also the color associated with money and wealth. Green, like the street light, stands for "go" and represents those who want to push ahead to succeed.

**Red-orange** is not a pure red. It has some yellow in it thereby giving it a bit of an orange feel and with it the feeling of energy. It represents vital forces of desire, appetite, and hunger and, as we have seen, is the favorite of fast-food restaurants. It also represents activity, and the person choosing this hue will be active and participate in sports and other physical activities. People choosing red in the first position want their own personal activities to be intense and want to experience life to the fullest and live it on the edge. It is also a color of strong sexual desire, but the ability to satisfy one's needs may be difficult. It is an intense hue and could be considered the "extreme color" as in extreme sports.

Bright yellow is the most saturated intense hue in the test and stands for sunny, bright, and happy thoughts. It represents the subject's desire for happiness. It may also represent someone who is going through a major personal crisis and wants and desires a happy outcome. Yellow is the color of haloes and gold and may have a religious significance or connotation. It represents the future, and the person who picks it is someone looking forward to the future and all it can bring.

Violet is composed of both red and blue and holds some of each color's association. Violet can represent someone who wants or sees a magical identification to the world with intimate and erotic overtones. When it is the first choice of children, it may mean they still find the world a magical place. An adult who chooses it in the first position may be both sensitive and unrealistic in their desires or goals.

Brown is a shade of orange representing sensations of the body and bodily functions. It is an earthy tone indicating the importance of home and feeling of belonging. It also may denote that the person selecting this shade may have feelings of unease and the desire to remedy a problem or situation.

Black is the darkest of all the colors in the test and is the negation or absence of all color. It represents the color of anarchy and protest; the person picking it wants to rebel against anything and everything. Those who choose black are those who do not to give up anything and may feel that things are not as they want them to be. It also denotes someone who may be pushing against fate and may do so just to be different and not do

what everyone else is doing—the dissenter and agitator. Black has an intense effect on the other colors chosen after it and is most normally picked in the last position.

Gray is a neutral; it is not a hue and is the midpoint in between black and white. It is not one thing or another and is free from all stimuli. It could be considered the DMZ color choice—not part of one thing or another. People selecting gray in the first position want to separate themselves from everyone and everything, walling themselves up. These people watch themselves go through the motions of daily life and are not involved. They prefer to stand alone stoically. Gray is statistically most often picked in sixth place in the test.

## The Brain and Cortex

We must remember that we do not pick out or decide on a color in isolation. Edwin Land,

**Figure 3-15.** An example of the retinex theory. The green stripe running down the center is actually the same color. It looks like two different hues of green due to the lightness or darkness of the corresponding background hues. We perceive color in relationship to the amount of light and the other hues surrounding it.

the inventor of the Polaroid camera, took this idea a step further with his **retinex theory.** Retinex is a combination of the words *retina* and *cortex*. He stated that colors are not determined in isolation and that colors change in relation to one another. We can take two swatches of the same color (in Figure 3-15, the chosen color is green), and depending upon the background color they are placed on, radically change their visual appearance. Johannes Itten and Joseph Albers demonstrated this theory in their works and were part of the traditional Bauhausian approach to teaching color theory.

In addition, Land said that even in the dark, we expect an object to retain its color. For example, we expect lemons to be yellow when we turn the lights off because we think we still see yellow even though the light has changed. This is another example of a learned response to color. Through a lifetime of experience, limes have always been green; therefore when we see a lime, we expect it to be green. No matter how the light changes, or the color surrounding the lime may change, we know the lime is green and that is exactly what we see. The brain and psyche ignore the reflected wavelength light impulses, overriding the incoming data, and decide based on years of knowledge of the color of the item. When we think of how we see, our first thought is of our eyes, but the mind and subconscious play a much more significant part in how we perceive color than we can imagine. The brain, in the end, may be the real arbiter of color.

## Summary

Whether it is the brain or the psyche that determines personal preferences, understanding the cultural and psychological implications of our color choices is vital in creating viable artwork and designs. Art is not created in a vacuum. People are influenced by their past experiences and by the culture in which they live. Every product, including the food we eat, has color added or enhanced in some manner. We have seen how color can change our feelings toward a product, making it look heavier, cheaper, or alter our sense of its net worth. Socioeconomic factors can also impact our color choices.

Psychoanalytic investigations of color usage help us to better understand ourselves and the emotional aspects of our lives. They can act as diagnostic tools in psychotherapy and aid the therapist or physician in treating a wide range of disorders. Future scientific investigations may yield a better understanding of how we perceive and respond to color and allow us a greater insight into the human condition.

Artists use color to imitate the effects of nature, such as the vanishing of mountains into the distance or atmosphere. Color can also be "heightened" to shock and add emotional impact. Understanding the viewer's psychological reaction to color enables the artist to achieve a desired response and create a more meaningful work of art. Designers choose the color of a product to elicit a response from viewers by taking into account their sex, age, and socioeconomic status. The goal is to match the color of the product to the customer or client.

Cultural aspects and associations with particular colors keep changing. Every culture may have its own color biases, but there are overriding psychological principles that cross all boundaries and are common to all people. It is the combination of all this knowledge that enables the artists and designers to better communicate their unique ideas. And above all, art and design is about communication.

**Color Harmonies: Chapter 4**

**Figure 4-1.**
Pablo Picasso, *Le vieux juif*, 1903.
© 2004 Estate of Pablo Picasso/Artists Rights Society (ARS), New York.
Picasso's use of blue was a physical manifestation in paint of his mental and emotional state. The major themes of the Blue Period paintings are all depressing subjects, including the blind, mental patients, madness, hunger, and melancholia. The canvas is cropped tightly to the figures, which produces a cramped, condensed space and adds to the bleak feeling of the painting.

rtists or designers rarely, if ever, work with one color alone, or dedicate themselves to only one hue. A few, like Picasso, may work with one dominant color for a period of time as he did in his Rose and Blue Periods (Figure 4-1). But this is the exception. Most work with many hues, and therefore, need to know how these various colors will interact with one another. Color harmonies, schemes, and color ways are synonymous terms, meaning the same thing. Rather than an artist trying different hues and having hit-or-miss results, color schemes are formulas or combinations that can be used to create a cohesive unified picture. These formulas are time-proven methods of using color to create a pleasing harmonic balance.

ACHROMATIC SCALE

**Figure 4-2.**
An example of an achromatic or value scale, also known as a gray scale.

The terms *hue*, *chrome*, and *color* are all names for the same thing. A **hue** is the actual, or proper, name of any given color. Today these words are interchanged with abandon, but as artists and designers, we must be more careful and accurate in our use of terminology. The term color tends to be more universal, while hue tends to be more specific and refers to a color found in the spectrum or on the color wheel.

### Shades of Gray

If all color is eliminated entirely, then what we would be left with is an **achromatic** range (Figure 4-2). We would be working with pure value or the lightness and darkness only without any hint of hue. In its most exacting definition, the prefix *a–* is from the Greek meaning not and "chroma" meaning color. In other words, it is without color or not colored. For something to be considered a hue or a color, it must have its own place or position on the color wheel. In theory, if you mixed all the hues on the color wheel, you would get black; however, it does not have its own place anywhere on the wheel. Using this definition, then black and white are not considered colors or hues. Along with the full range of grays, black and white are neutrals. Therefore, they are not hues or colors and should never be referred to as such. This sometimes gets confusing because in daily life people often refer to black, white, or even gray as colors. Artists and designers need to be specific in their use of language. In my own work, as seen in Figure 4-3, I combine digitally created images that have been altered and worked into with graphite

to produce an achromatic image. The only addition of color is the added mixed media souvenir items. Their spot color adds a visual contrast and counterpoint to the black-and-white images and aids in establishing a focal point in the artwork.

Each hue has its corresponding, or related, value. This is known as **inherent value.** Understanding this relation of each hue and its corresponding value assists the artist and designer in developing and setting up color

**Figure 4-3.**
Steven Bleicher, *Mobil Special (from the Route 66 Series),* 2001. Even limited color acts like a magnet. The viewer's eye is first drawn to the colored souvenir item, which then leads into the rest of the work.

**Figure 4-4.**
An example of a
relational hue and
value scale. If you
squint your eyes, the line
between the hue and its
relative value should
begin to disappear.

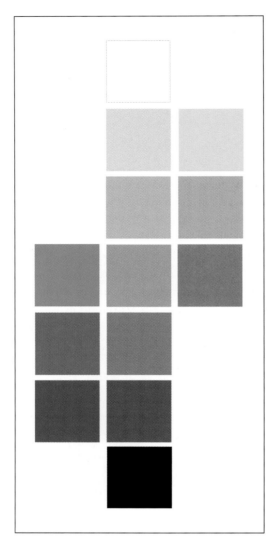

harmonies. There is no direct correlation of
white to a hue. It is too light in value and
even the most bright intense yellow would
be darker, which is why yellow starts off our
relational value and hue scale as a light gray,
as seen in Figure 4-4. As we move up the
scale, red and green tend to match each other
in their relative value at middle gray. Blues
and violets make up the darker end of the
scale as deep grays. Just as white has no
equivalent hue, neither does black. It's too
dark. Even the deepest violet would still be
lighter in value than black. In essence, black
is the absence of all color and is the darkest
value possible.

**Tints, Tones, and Shades**

The most simple color harmony possible
is a **monochromatic** scheme. *Mono–* comes
from the Greek for one, meaning that it is
a schema that is comprised only of a single
hue. As shown in Figure 4-5, it is the full
range of a color from its lightest tint to its
deepest shade and everything in between,
but it is always one very specific hue. A **tint**
is the hue plus the addition of white. We often
think of them as pastel colors, soft and full of
light. If a hue is mixed with gray, a **tone** is
created. The base gray mixed with the hue

**Figure 4-5.**
An example of three
monochromatic scales:
blue, yellow, and orange.
The pure hue is at the
center and the shades of
each are shown on the
left, while the tints are
displayed on the right.
Notice that, depending
upon the hue, the addi-
tion of black creates
surprising results.
If black is mixed with
yellow, the shade
appears to have a
greenish cast, while
if black is mixed with
orange, it creates brown.

MONOCHROMATIC SCALES

can be very light to extremely dark and everything in between the full range. It may be the widest range of the three components that comprise a monochromatic scheme. Mixing black with the hue will produce a **shade** of that color. You can vary the intensity of the shade depending upon which type of black paint is used in its creation. Ivory Black creates a transparent warm shade, while Lamp Black will produce an opaque warm shade. On the other hand, Mars and Oxide Black produce cool shades. So even in something as simple as this, there can be great complexity.

To illustrate this point more clearly, Figure 4-6 shows what can happen if one specific hue, such as red, is made into a tint and shade. If red is mixed with white to make a tint, the resulting color is pink. On the other hand, if black is added to the hue, maroon is the result. Yet it is still red—the hue has not changed and remains constant. Various tints and shades of red are used in Victor Rodriguez's *Gordo* (Figure 4-7). The shades create depth and shadow and give the

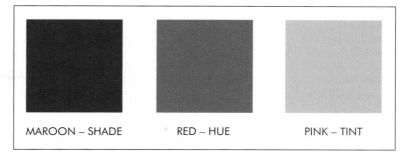

| MAROON – SHADE | RED – HUE | PINK – TINT |

face its form. The tints are used in contrast to focus the viewers' attention on the figure entering the mouth. The darker values visually recede into the background, while the tints appear to advance to the foreground.

Many artists have worked with monochromatic compositions, though Pablo Picasso may be the most famous. His decision to use blue was not because (as some stories have suggested) he could only afford blue paint, but directly related to the severe depression he sank into after the death of his best friend. However, not all use of blue represents sadness or depression. Mimi Shapiro, a well-known contemporary artist,

**Figure 4-6.**
An illustration of the range of a monochromatic red hue. The base hue is red and when mixed with white, it creates a tint, in this case pink. If the same red hue is mixed with black, a shade is created, namely maroon. Regardless of whether it is a tint or a shade, the hue is still red.

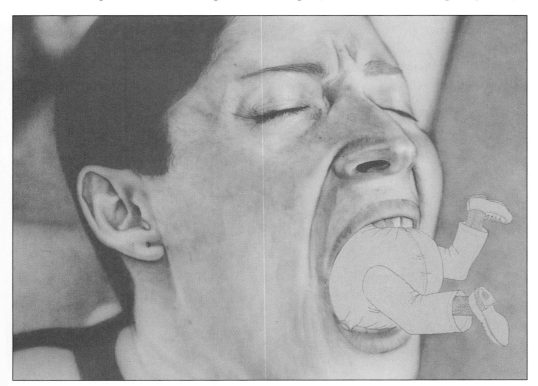

**Figure 4-7.**
Victor Rodriguez, *Gordo*, 1997. (Courtesy of Yvanamor Palix Space d'Art, Paris, France.)
A single hue of color can be used for its emotional content. Here the red used is bright and vibrant. Rodriguez uses the pure hue and tints, but very few shades. This intense color palette intensifies the shocking nature of the images.

uses a monochrome blue range in her book-art piece, *The Poet's Dream* (Figure 4-8). Here the blue hue is used to produce an ethereal mood. As with the Rodriguez painting, the dark hues create a background while the tints create a foreground. The actual cutouts of the pages in Shapiro's work constitute an additional layer of shadow and value working in low relief.

### Hue, Value, and Saturation

There are three components that artists consider when working with color. They are hue, value, and saturation. Each can be controlled and will have a significant impact on how the hue may be viewed. When choosing a hue from a color wheel or spectrum, an artist is making a specific color choice. For example, blue is a different hue than blue-green or blue-violet. The value of the hue can be changed or adjusted as needed, and more white or black can be added as required.

The final component is **saturation** or the intensity and purity of the given hue. Another way to think of saturation is as the brightness or dullness of a color. Brighter, more intense colors usually denote a purer saturation of the particular hue. Any hue can be desaturated to make it appear more gray, drab, and dingy in appearance (Figure 4-9). When we look at the hues on the color wheel, we see the purest, most saturated form of the hue. Altering the saturation can drastically change our perception of the image and even make it hard to look

**Figure 4-9.**
An example of the desaturation of the hue red. As the color becomes increasingly more desaturated, it loses its red color and becomes more gray and washed out.

at (Figure 4-10). Bright super-saturated hues can be great attention grabbers, but they can be hard to look at for any length of time.

## The Color Wheel

The circular format of the color wheel will now become more useful and meaningful. The specific placement of the hues along the circumference of the wheel will help illustrate the relationships or harmonies. First, each hue is spaced an equal distance from each other. A color wheel can have as few as six hues and then doubles itself as more hues are distinguished. The next and most commonly used would be the twelve-step color wheel (Figure 4-11), but you could also have twenty-four- and forty-eight-step versions as well. Color wheels must always have an even number of hues and that number must be divisible by three. Any other combination would not be a true and accurate color wheel.

The color wheel is comprised of three primary colors, or **primaries:** yellow, red, and blue. Primaries are so named because they cannot be broken down any further and are the principal ingredients that make up all other colors. If you mix equal parts of two primary hues, a **secondary** hue is created. There are only three secondaries: orange, green, and violet. Blue and yellow make green, blue and red make violet or purple, and yellow and red make orange. If primary and secondary hues are mixed, an **intermediate** or **tertiary** hue is created.

On the standard twelve-step color wheel there are six intermediates: yellow-orange, yellow-green, blue-green, blue-violet, red-violet, and red-orange. On larger color wheels, intermediate hues can be mixed with primary or secondary hues to create **quaternary** colors.

## Color Temperature

The color wheel can be divided into two basic areas, or groups, of warm and cool hues. The warm range is comprised of yellow, orange, red, and some hues of green. The cool hues normally include everything from blue-green to the various forms of blues and violets. However, there are few absolutes when dealing with color. Color is relative and will change depending upon the other hues placed next to them or in close proximity, as seen in

WARM

COOL

**Figure 4-10.**
The center image of the flower is shown at its normal hue and saturation. Its even tones of red and green create a normal-looking picture and are pleasing to the eye. The image on the left is desaturated. It has lost most of its color and there is only a hint of color peeking out of the gray. The picture on the right is super-saturated. Using Adobe Photoshop, the color saturation of the image was enhanced, increasing the intensity of the hues. The colors are so intense they begin to vibrate and jump off the page and are hard to look at for any length of time. Pumping up the saturation of an image can be used to grab the viewer's attention or to create a focal point.

**Figure 4-11.**
An example of a twelve-step color wheel. Each hue is spaced at equal distances from each other.

**Figure 4-12.**
An example of the relationship between warm and cool hues. In the top row, the base color, or squares, are warm, and the circles are cool. In the second row, the base colors are cool, and the circles are warm in relation to the color of the square. Therefore, a hue such as green can be warm in relation to blue, but cool when compared to yellow-green.

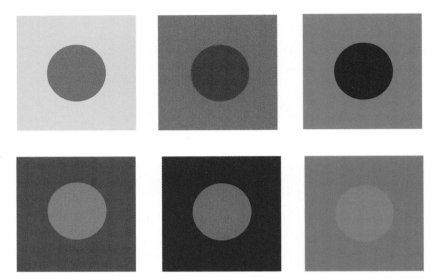

Figure 4-12. For example, yellow may be warm in relation to blue-green, but blue-green may be warm in relation to violet. Green may be cool in relation to another warm hue such as yellow-orange, but considered warm when it is placed next to blue-violet.

Color temperature can also be used to create spatial effects. Visually, warm hues appear to advance on the picture plane. They seem to move toward us and give the feeling of the color coming out toward the viewer. Cool hues have the opposite effect. They appear to recede into space on the picture plane. These are very important concepts for artists and designers to remember when working with color.

Franz Marc used this spatial phenomenon in *Siberian Dogs in the Snow* (Figure 4-13). He worked with a limited color palette comprised almost exclusively of white, blue, and yellow. The warmer yellow hues are used

**Figure 4-13.**
Franz Marc. *Siberian Dogs in the Snow*. Gift of Mr. and Mrs. Stephen M. Kellen, Image © 2004 Board of Trustees, National Gallery of Art, Washington, 1909/10. Marc uses warm hues to bring elements of the painting closer to the viewer. Cool hues are used as shadows to give depth to the painting, since cool hues recede into space. Bright yellow is used to show the lightest highlight, and tints of the same hue are used to create a middle ground, along with the tints of blue. Shades of blue are used to create deep shadows.

as highlights and appear to advance on the picture plane. The white becomes a base, or ground, while the blues are used in the shadows. The cool hues recede into the background, which allows the white dogs to stand out against the snow.

## More Spatial Effects

Atmospheric perspective is another method of using color to create spatial effects. As objects move farther away from the viewer (or foreground), they lose color. In fact, not only do they become desaturated as they recede in space, the farther back the objects are from the foreground, the less texture and detail that will be visible. As shown in Figure 4-14, the less light illuminating the objects, the less color, texture, and detail that can be seen. Colors do not, as most people think, dissolve into black in the background. In actuality, they fade out into a middle gray. Just look out

at any scene where you have a great expanse or can see a far distance, and you will notice that as things recede into space, they lose their color and become blurred.

## Transparency and Space

When working with color, we tend to think about working with solid opaque areas of color. Dense applications or sections of color will work the same way that shapes work in creating spatial relationships. If two solid shapes of color overlap one another, the top shape will appear to be in front of the other shape. This is the traditional concept of overlapping elements defining spatial relationships. However, if the sector where the two patches of color overlap is transparent, then it is nearly impossible to tell which is in front of the other. This creates an arbitrary or ambiguous sense of space. For a hue to look transparent, the middle hue must be a visual mixture and

**Figure 4-14.**
Diane Blazy, *Blue Ridge Mountains*, 2001. Diane Blazy's photograph of the Blue Ridge Mountains is a perfect example of atmospheric perspective. The warmth of the green hues creates the appearance of a foreground. As we look off into the distance, the green color becomes desaturated gradually moving from deep green to a cool blue gray. The mountaintops dissolve into a neutral as they move farther back in space.

**Figure 4-15.**
An example of transparency and how it affects spatial relationships. In the image on the left, the middle ground of the yellow-green allows the illusion of the cylinder to flip back and forth. In the image on the right, the solid areas of yellow and green give us a fixed and constant view of the cylinder.

middle ground of the two hues expressed. This can be achieved through a middle mixture of hue or value within the same hue. This is one of the underlying concepts that allows artists to create many optical illusions (Figure 4-15).

The material an artist uses may also create transparent or translucent effects. Watercolors and thin washes of oil paint are transparent. Many other materials can also have diaphanous qualities creating visual illusions of space. Peter Zimmermann used plastics in *Pantone* (Figure 4-16). Here the material gives the work its transparent quality. As layers of plastic are built up, more opaque colors will appear. In addition, the see-through nature of material can further be enhanced by the use of lighter hues. The lighter the hue (or tint) of the material used, the more translucent it will be. Conversely, the darker the material, the more opaque and dense the effect that will be achieved.

## Color Harmonies

Color harmonies, color ways, and color schemes are all different terms for the same thing. They are the ways in which artists and designers pick and use a combination of hues, knowing that they will work together in a composition. In a sense, they take the guesswork out of choosing color. These harmonies can easily be seen in their

**Figure 4-16.**
Peter Zimmermann, *Pantone*, 2002.
© 2004 Artists Rights Society (ARS),
New York/VG Bild-Kunst, Bonn.
Zimmermann uses the transparent nature of the epoxy resin to create overlapping planes of color. It is virtually impossible to begin to figure out which layer of color is on top of the other. This creates an amorphous sense of space that constantly fluctuates between foreground and middle ground. Only the white background seems somewhat constant. What do you think?

relationships to each other on the color wheel. These relationships reinforce the importance of why hues are placed in a circular format.

The most closely associated color way or harmony is an **analogous** color scheme. An analogous group is any three hues directly next to each other on the color wheel (Figure 4-17). In the twelve-step color wheel, yellow-green, green, and blue-green are analogous. As the color wheel gets larger, the range within an analogous grouping can become much more limited. In some large wheels with more than twelve steps, the range is sometimes increased to four hues next to each other. The key is that they are always directly next to each other. This color scheme has the least contrast. Because the colors are so close in hue, they almost seem to blend into one another and can make differentiating form more difficult. This is especially true in the cooler range of hues.

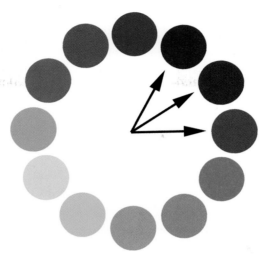

**Figure 4-17.**
A color wheel showing an analogous color scheme of red-violet, violet, and blue-violet. These are the same cool hues used in James Turrell's *To be Sung*.

We tend to think of these color ways as working only with paint and pigments, but they are also used in other forms of art, from performance to conceptual art. James Turrell used an analogous scheme in *To be Sung* (Figure 4-18). The cool hues add to the emotional aspects of the work.

**Figure 4-18.**
James Turrell, *To be Sung,* 1994. Still photograph of a live performance. Turrell uses an analogous color scheme of red-violet, violet, and blue-violet. These hues create a cool, dark mood in his performance piece, adding to its evocative nature.

### Vanishing Boundaries

If two hues are very similar to each other in value and saturation, they will have a dramatic visual impact and interaction with each other. Where the two hues meet, the line or boundary between them appears to vanish (Figure 4-19). This effect is common when working with analogous schemes or with colors that are very close in value or saturation. This visual result can be achieved with both bright and dull hues alike; all that matters is that the hues must be close in value and intensity.

To eliminate this visual blending, simply change one of the colors, and make it either darker or lighter than the other hue or adjust the saturation. In either case, the object is to create a higher level of contrast, thereby eliminating the effect. Mark Rothko purposely created paintings that used the concept of vanishing boundaries as a key element in some of his work (Figure 4-20). At first glance, the painting looks as if it is two-toned—red and black. The areas of deep, intense dark blue are not noticeable. Upon closer examination, the viewer can pick out the thin blue area surrounding the red rectangle. The influence of Albers's color studies is clearly evident in Rothko's work and use of color.

**Figure 4-19.**
An illustration of the principle of vanishing boundaries. Notice that the two squares in the larger blue box are barely visible. They are close in value and saturation to the larger square and seem to blend into the background.

**Figure 4-20.**
Mark Rothko, *Maroon on Blue*, 1957-60.
© Kate Rothko Prizel & Christopher Rothko/
Artists Rights Society (ARS), New York.
The edge where the deep blue meets the black seems to dissolve and disappear. This is due in part to the inherent value of the blue, which is very dark and nearly black in value. The vibrant red appears to be luminous because it is the lightest and brightest part of the canvas, and it creates a counterpoint to the dark blue and back areas.

## Complements

Two colors that are exactly opposite from each other on the color wheel are known as **complements** (Figure 4-21). They represent the highest form of contrast within the color wheel. If the hues picked are equal in value and saturation and are placed next to each other in a design, the colors will appear to vibrate. They will also appear to be brighter and more intense. This is also known as **complementary contrast.** Complementary contrast is a reaction in the viewer's eye and not with the actual pigments. The cones within the eye are not at rest and the visual color vibration is the result. They could also be thought of as a balance between warm and cool colors.

In any complementary pair, one hue will be warm and the other cool. The Impressionists and Postimpressionists were masters of the use of complementary pairs in their works. This is one of the reasons why the colors in their canvases are so bright and vivid and have an atmospheric, luminescent quality. A more modern example of this can be seen in Figure 4-22, a *Study After Velazquez's Portrait of Pope Innocent X* by Francis Bacon. Here the yellow and violet contrast, intensify, and heighten each other. By placing these against the very dark background, the image seems to float on the picture plane.

**Figure 4-21.**
A color wheel showing a complementary color scheme of yellow and violet. These are the same complements Francis Bacon used in his *Study after Velazquez's Portrait of Pope Innocent X.* Complementary hues work together and intensify each other. These are eye-catching color combinations, which are also frequently used in graphic design.

**Figure 4-22.**
Francis Bacon, *Study after Velazquez's Portrait of Pope Innocent X,* 1953.
© 2004 Estate of Francis Bacon/ARS, New York/DACS, London.
Bacon uses the complementary pair of yellow and violet. The use of complements intensifies the two hues and creates the effect of the figure floating on the background. They are so bold in their visual effect that we almost fail to notice the pale tint of orange in the picture. The use of warm hues also moves those elements to the foreground of the composition.

**Figure 4-23.**
Jasper Johns, *Flag*, 1965.
© Jasper Johns/
Licensed by VAGA,
New York, NY.
Johns's painting illus-
trates the concept of
successive contrast or
afterimage. Stare at the
white dot on the flag for
40 seconds and then
look at the black dot on
the bottom rectangle.
You should see the flag
in its correct colors.

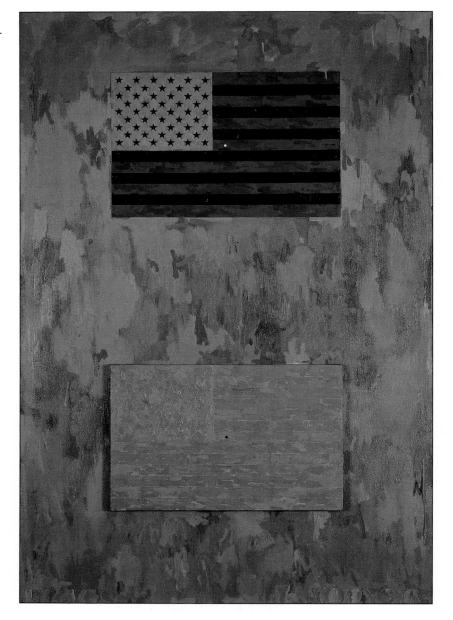

As we have seen in the previous chapter, another phenomenon caused by viewing one half of a complementary pair is that it causes the cones in the eye to be overstimulated. If the person then looks at a white or neutral color, the other half of the complement pair will appear or will show up as an afterimage (Figure 4-23). This action is also known as **successive contrast.** Jasper Johns used this phenomenon in his painting, *Flag*. If you stare intensely at the green and black flag for about 40 seconds, and then look below it at the black point, you will see an afterimage of the flag in red, white, and blue.

Two hues directly opposite each other on the color wheel are the most simple and fundamental use of complementary colors. But there are more intricate and elaborate variations. In a **split complement** (Figure 4-24) instead of selecting both opposites, one end is selected and at the other end the two colors adjacent are picked.

They form an upside down "Y" shape or one that resembles a peace symbol without the center leg. The additional color gives the artist more material to work with and allows for more complexity in design. Alexander Calder used these colors in his *Stabile-Mobile* (Figure 4-25) to heighten the brilliance of the hues and create a more dynamic structure.

In a **double split complementary** color scheme, two colors next to each other and their two corresponding complements are selected (Figure 4-26). This allows for an even greater variation and complexity in design.

### Neutrals

If two complements are mixed together, they form a **neutral** (Figure 4-27). When white is added to a neutral, it becomes almost gray in color. The Impressionists used this technique to make grays and tone down

or desaturate hues. Unlike the flat gray produced by adding white to black, the artist can use this process to develop either warm-based grays or cool-based grays. Romare Bearden (Figure 4-28) uses a neutral mixture of blue and orange, as well as shades of orange, to create a full range of browns in

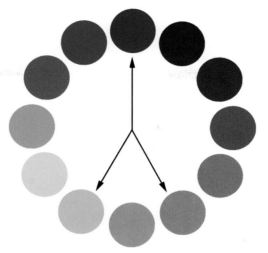

**Figure 4-24.**
A color wheel showing a split complement color scheme of blue, yellow-orange, and red-orange has the same hues used in the sculpture by Alexander Calder in *Stabile-Mobile.*

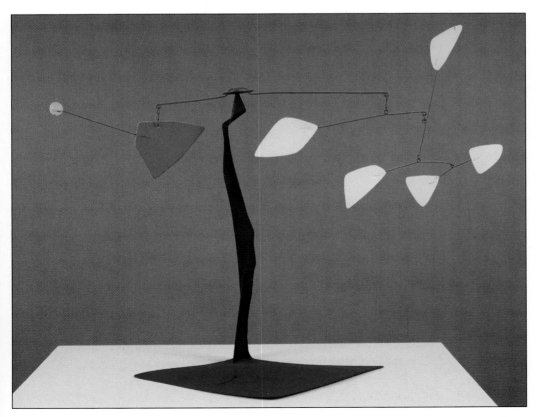

**Figure 4-25.**
Alexander Calder, *Stabile-Mobile,* 1972. ©2004 Estate of Alexander Calder/Artists Rights Society (ARS), New York, NY. Photo Credit: Art Resource, New York. Calder uses a split complement to create a more complex color scheme within a limited range.

**Figure 4-26.**
A color wheel showing a double split complement scheme of yellow and violet paired up with the neighboring pair of yellow-green and red-violet.

**Figure 4-27.**
The illustration shows three sets of complements— red/green, orange/blue, and violet/yellow— blending into one another to create their respective neutrals.

**Figure 4-28.**
Romare Bearden, *Early Morning,* 1964. © Romare Bearden Foundation/Licensed by VAGA, New York, NY. Tate Gallery, London/Art Resource, New York. Bearden uses neutralizations of blue and orange as the dominant color scheme in his mixed media creation by using both collaged elements and paint. The brighter orange hues are used as highlights and visually advance on the picture plane to create a warm foreground.

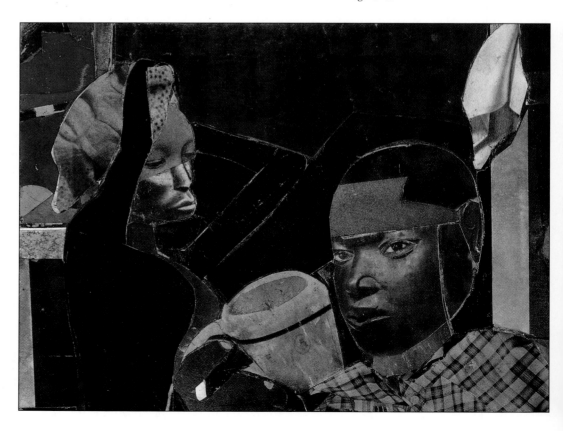

his composition, *Early Morning*. The picture tells a narrative story of a young man preparing to start a long day of work on the farm. Much of Bearden's work is autobiographical and, as in this piece, evokes memories of the artist's early childhood. His collage work also has a cubist influence, which is especially recognizable in the patterning of the boy's shirt and shifting planes or views of the table.

## Triads

Like the name implies, a **triad** is composed of three hues. Each of these hues must be of equal distance from the other on the color wheel (Figure 4-29). Another way for us to remember the makeup of a triad is to think of it as an equilateral triangle placed inside of the wheel or the shape of a Mercedes-Benz hood ornament. Each color or location touched by a point of the triangle would represent a hue. The most common and simplest form of this color scheme would be the three primary hues or the three secondary hues. But intermediate hues can also make up a triad. Roy Lichtenstein used a triad in *As I Opened Fire* (Figure 4-30). The intensely saturated primary hues add to the graphic nature of the piece and are reminiscent of action hero comic books. The simple bold

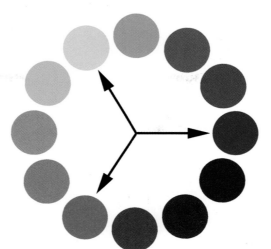

**Figure 4-29.**
A color wheel showing a triad. Here yellow, red, and blue (which are also the primary hues) make up the simplest grouping of three hues equally spaced apart from one another. These are the same hues used in Lichtenstein's *As I Opened Fire*. Secondary or intermediate hues can also make up a triad.

**Figure 4-30.**
Roy Lichtenstein, *As I Opened Fire*, 1964.
Stedelijk Museum, Amsterdam.
Lichtenstein used a limited color palette of flat simple hues in most of his work. In *As I Opened Fire,* he uses a triadic color scheme of primary hues to create harmony between the images. The use of this color scheme acts as a unifying element and brings the three canvases that make up the composition (or triptych) together as a whole. Within the triad, tints and shades of the hues may be used, as long as the color remains visually within the tricolor schema. In this piece, Lichtenstein uses a tone of red in all three panels. This allows the artist a wider range of color choices within this limited hue grouping.

**Figure 4-31.**
A color wheel showing a tetrad color scheme. This tetrad consists of yellow-green, orange, blue, and red-violet.

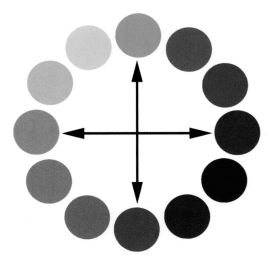

use of unmodulated color and elements from popular culture were thematic of Pop art. The secondary hues can also make up a triadic group. You could pick three intermediate colors to form a triad, as long as they are spaced an equal distance from one another. The real variable factor is how many steps or hues comprise the color wheel you are using as reference, and that the hues selected are spaced the same distance from each other.

## Tetrads

If a square were placed inside the color wheel, each of the corners of the box would touch upon a hue. The hues touched on create or form a **tetrad** (Figure 4-31). Like

a triad, each hue must be an equal distance from one another. A tetrad will always consist of one set of complements made up of a primary and a secondary hue, as well as two intermediate hues for the second pair of complements. Of all of the color ways, the tetrad offers the artist the greatest range of hues and contrast to work with.

## The Bezold Effect

Wilhem von Bezold was a scientist involved in textile production. In his work with weavers, he noticed that if one color was changed in a design, it could have a radical effect on the overall composition and feeling of the design. By changing the dominant hue in a pattern, the entire composition could be modified, as illustrated in Figure 4-32. While this effect is most easily recognizable in a pattern, the concept will work in any composition where you have multiple or repeated images of the same subject. By changing a dominant color, the appearance of shapes and their relationships to each other can alter the overall composition. This is the power and strength of color.

## Simultaneous Contrast

Our perception of color is affected by the environment in which we see that hue. Because a color is rarely seen by itself,

**Figure 4-32.**
An illustration of the Bezold effect. By changing the dominant hue in a design or artwork, the artist can completely change its look and feel. In this example, the design is the same; only the blue diamonds have been changed to yellow, producing a dramatically different effect.

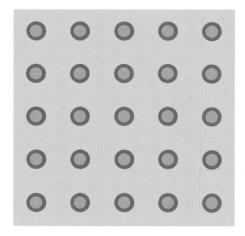

the surrounding colors will influence and, in many cases, alter the color perceived. This visual phenomenon is known as **simultaneous contrast** and occurs when one color is seen on differing backgrounds. It is commonly associated with complements, but it can also occur in any situation when two or more hues are placed next to each other. This is because the appearance of color is relative and is always affected by the surrounding hues. For example, when a hue of yellow is placed next to a neutral gray, as seen in Figure 4-33, the gray will appear to have a cool or violet cast to it. If that same gray is then placed on a violet ground, it will have a warm or yellowish cast to it. A similar color transformation will occur if we place the same midvalue red hue on contrasting backgrounds, as seen in the lower half of Figure 4-33. The hue in the square literally seems to change color. On the darker background, the midvalue color will appear lighter than it really is, and on the light background, the opposite will occur. In addition, when two hues of equal value and intensity are placed next to each other, they tend to cause a visual vibration at the edges where they meet. This intensifies each hue.

There is an illustrious story of an interior designer working for a famous movie star (who we will leave nameless). The movie star hated yellow or any hue with any type of a yellow tinge to it. She wanted her new home decorated in various hues, shades, and tints of violet, the color of royalty. The interior designer went to work creating the new furnishings. Months later the actor toured her new home and then angrily called the designer, upset by the yellow-toned carpet selected. The interior designer was stunned; he had ordered a light, neutral gray carpet and even checked his invoices to make sure the correct flooring was delivered. So what went wrong? The

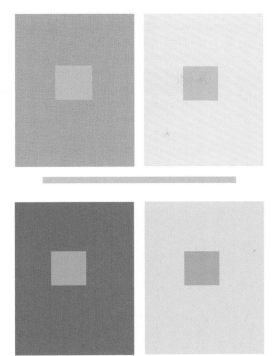

designer forgot the law of simultaneous contrast. The light gray carpet appeared to have a hint of yellow when it was surrounded by all of the various hues of violet. The viewer's eye automatically placed the complement hue in the neutral (gray carpet) and visually turned it into a yellow tone. This is the same concept shown in the previous example. It really was nothing more than a trick of the eye.

**Figure 4-33.**
An illustration of two forms of simultaneous contrast. In the top example, a neutral gray is placed on two complementary backgrounds. The gray square seems to be completely different, depending upon the hue of the background. In the bottom example, the same red hue as seen in the stripe below it is placed on contrasting red backgrounds. Although they are the same color, the red square appears to be very different in each. This is an important concept to keep in mind when working with color.

**Figure 4-34.**
In this illustration, when the blue square is surrounded by the black outline, it condenses the color and form making it look smaller than the square surrounded by the white. The blue square with the white border seems to be larger, visually encroaching into the white area.

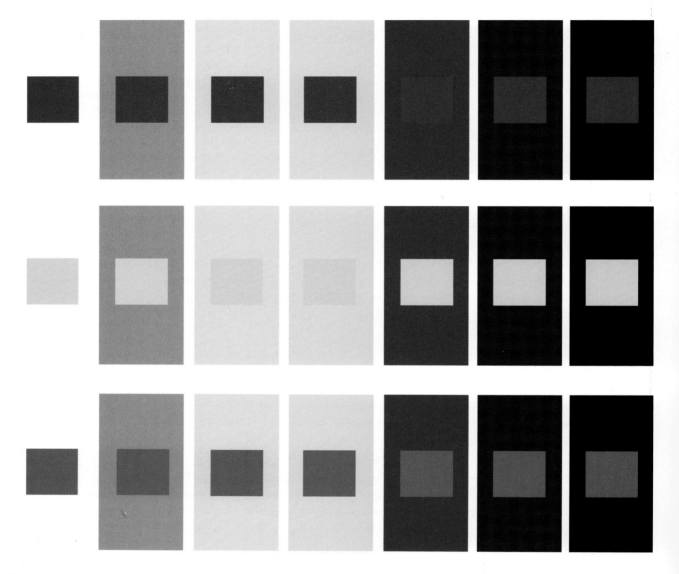

**Figure 4-35.**
An example of value contrast. Notice how the color changes, depending upon the value and temperature of the background hue.

## Interactions of Black and White

Most of the color studies and interactions we have observed so far deal with one color placed next to or on top of another. For these reactions to occur, the hues in question must be placed directly next to or on top of each other. This is because colors react quite differently when surrounded by either black or white, as demonstrated in Figure 4-34. If a color is seen against a black outline, it frames the hue and constrains its visual presence. It is as if the black frame is holding the hue in and compressing it. But if the color is viewed against a white outline, the hue seems to visually expand into the white area. Even though the white boundary isolates the hue from the background, it allows the color to visually swell into its space.

## Value Contrast

Closely related to simultaneous contrast is the concept of **value contrast.** One of the easiest ways to change the look of a color is to place it on a contrasting background. Colors may appear very different, depending upon the background they are placed on or next to, as illustrated in Figure 4-35. Placing a hue on a dark background isolates it and makes it appear lighter, and it also makes the lighter hue appear larger. Conversely, placing the same colored hue on a light background makes it look darker and smaller. However, there is no reaction if the background and foreground colors are of equal value. There must be a contrast between the hues to achieve this effect.

## Luminosity and Luminescence

Another element in the appearance of light and color is **luminosity.** Luminosity is the perceived light given off by an object and goes hand in hand with value. In artistic terms, it most often refers to the lightest part of an image and can be created through the use of high contrast lighting such as chiaroscuro. Contrasting a bright, intense hue off a darker, less saturated cooler hue will also produce a similar effect.

As seen previously in Figure 4-20, Mark Rothko's work was renowned for its luminous quality. In *Maroon on Blue,* the loosely constructed red rectangle seems to glow. By placing the form on a very dark, warm background and outlining it with a very thin, intense cool blue, the red area becomes a focal point. Because it is the lightest and most saturated color, it appears to advance on the picture plane and exhibits a shimmering quality. The more light that appears to be emitted by the colors or

object, the closer it will seem to the viewer and the brighter the effect will be. The brightness decreases as its source moves back on the picture plane and is farther away from the viewer.

Luminosity can also be created through the use of actual lighting (or use of lamps) within the work of art, as seen in Figure 4-36. The light given off by the object can be measured in candles or candelas; however, in artistic terms it is not thought of as a measurable or quantifiable element. It is the objective measurement of the brightness of a surface that is reflecting or transmitting light. In more technical terms, luminescence is the emanation of light from a source that is not hot enough or does not produce enough heat to be incandescent like a light bulb. Bioluminescence refers to the light emitted by a living organism, most normally insects or fish. If you think of the firefly, the light produced in its tail section is an excellent example of bioluminescence.

## Summary

Color harmonies afford the artist and the designer set rules for choosing colors. They take the guesswork out of hue selection and give the artist some guidelines for their use. The color wheel is central to understanding these relationships. Color harmonies are

**Figure 4-36.**
Toby Archer, *Dawn Horizon,* 1995. In Archer's work, the luminous quality of the work is created by the use of neon light. The lamps give off a soft glow that expands out onto the picture plane. Unlike the visual luminescence in Rothko's work, here Archer works with actual light.

established based on the relationship of one hue to another and the corresponding position of the hues on the wheel. The wheel can also be divided into warm and cool hues, but the visual temperature of any given color is relative and may change depending on the hue selected for comparison.

Color can also create spatial relationships. The proper use of a color can make things look bigger or smaller, lighter or heavier. If the hues are close in value or intensity, it can blur the boundary between the two color areas. Colors can be made to appear transparent by selecting or mixing a visual middle or mixture of the two main hues.

Due to the complex interaction of colors to one another, you must take great care in selecting them. Your specific choices can make or break the design or desired effect. By understanding the interplay of color mixtures and combinations, you will be able to create more complex, evocative, and effective artworks and designs.

## Pigments, Colorants, and Paints: Chapter 5

**A**rt-making began as the first prehistoric humans took charred sticks from the fire and began to scratch markings onto a rock or cave wall (Figure 5-1). Through trial and error, or maybe purely by accident, these individuals found that the grease from their hands or the liquid from their saliva made the charcoal adhere better to the rough surface. Not only did it bond to the surface more easily, but it flowed in a smoother, more graceful manner. This could be one explanation of how the first mediums or binders were created to aid in the application of color.

As these early humans looked around at their environment, they soon realized that other things—such as plants, earth, and clay—could be ground up and mixed with these liquids to add color to the black outlines. This mixture of simple coloring agents formed the most rudimentary pigments. Through imagination and experimentation, they found new minerals, plants, and animal products to produce an even wider range of hues. Ever since that day, artists, designers, chemists, and dyers have been on a quest to find new pigments to create a wider array of colors.

Today we have many choices of materials and mediums to work with, including oils, acrylics, and watercolors. Artists can choose to work with color in a stick form with pastels, colored pencils, and markers. The computer has opened up a whole new range of color media possibilities with a wide variety of inks available to use in the printing process. There are dyes for cloth and fabrics. And there are even more nontraditional coloring agents used for body decoration and tattooing. Artists should experiment with

**Figure 5-1.**
Cave painting, Hall of Bulls, Lascaux, France. Cave Painting in Lascaux, circa 15,000 B.C. Since the dawn of time, people have been experimenting with a variety of minerals, plants, and other elements to create pigments and paints. This urge to express ourselves seems to be inherent and a unique quality of our human experience.

**Figure 5-2.**
The history of the paint tube from the early 1800s to 1905. Before the advent of the metal tube in 1840, paints were sold in pig bladders. They had a tendency to dry out easily and were very delicate to work with. The metal paint tube allowed artists to leave the confines of the studio and paint on location. Courtesy of Winsor & Newton.

a variety of media to find the ones they are most comfortable with and that can best express their unique vision.

## A Short History

Dating back to the earliest recorded artworks such as the cave paintings found in southern Europe, the images created show a limited range of hues. Reds, yellows, earth tones, and black dominated the prehistoric palette. These colors were derived from clay, minerals, and burnt or charred animal bones. Animal fats, saliva, and even urine were used as vehicles to aid in the application and adhesion of the colorants.

James Rand invented the first paint tubes (as we know them today) in 1840. Prior to this, artists' paints were sold or stored in pig bladders, which are similar to the natural casings used in making sausage (Figure 5-2). They were bulky and hard to work with. Imagine having to carry your paints around in something as fragile and awkward as a sausage. Two years later, Winsor & Newton began marketing and selling its paint in these new tubes. This was the time of the industrial revolution, which also brought other new innovations to the art world. New hues were developed and mass produced including cerulean blue in 1860 and alizarin a few years later in 1868. These new hues had

a profound impact on the Impressionists who were quick to pick up on and use these new colors. Artists have always been interested in new technology as it relates to making art, and the Impressionists were no different. Some of the variety and intensity of the colors found in their work can be directly attributed to the new paints being developed and produced during this time.

## Pigments

Paints are made up of two basic parts: a pigment and a vehicle. **Pigments** (Figure 5-3) are the powdered agents or elements that make up the colored part or hue of the paint. They can be made from a wide range of natural materials, including flowers, plants, and minerals such as oxides. Today many

**Figure 5-3.**
Dry powder pigments. Pigments are the agents that give paints, pastels, and inks their color. Courtesy of Winsor & Newton.

companies use synthetic or artificial colorants. Whatever the pigment is, it must be ground up as finely as possible so that each particle can be completely coated with the vehicle. The finer the pigment can be ground, the better the vehicle can surround and coat each tiny particle.

### Vehicles

The **vehicle** is a liquid or gel that combines with the pigment and suspends it in solution for application. It should completely coat each molecule of pigment and allow it to move and flow freely and evenly. During the Middle Ages, egg yoke and water were used as transporting agents for tempera. Each medium has it own vehicle. Oil paint, as the name suggests, uses oil as a vehicle—normally linseed, walnut, or safflower oil. Acrylics use plastic polymers, and watercolor uses gum arabic. This means that you cannot mix one type of paint with another because their vehicles are different; for example, you

can't mix watercolors with oil paints. Since oil and water don't mix, there is no common transportation agent.

### Professional Grade Versus Student Grade

If you go into any art supply store, you will find a vast selection of brands of paints by several different manufacturers. Golden, Winsor & Newton, Liquitex, Grumbacher and many more companies fill the shelves with their products. Even within one manufacturer there can be several categories or grades of paint, each with their own subbrand name. Some grades are more expensive than others. Artist or professional series paints cost more than student grades, and there can even be lesser grades for hobbyists and children.

So why are there so many different grades of paint? One of the first considerations is the paint archival or the number of years it will stay true to its color. As a professional artist or designer, you want to be sure that for years to come the hue will remain constant and true without fading, yellowing, cracking, or decomposing with age. The student or hobbyist may not really care if fifty years from now the painting degenerates with the passing of time.

Along with archivability is the amount and quality of the actual pigments used. The higher the quality and greater amount of pigment, the more expensive it will be. Many low-cost paints use synthetic colorants. The genuine cadmiums of professional grade paints may be replaced by less costly "hues," which are created by using a mixture of several pigments to approximate the color of the pure cadmium.

Another reason paints can vary in price is the manufacturing process itself. The finer the pigment is milled or ground, the more expensive it will be (Figure 5-4). In the highest quality paints, the mixture may have

**Figure 5-4.**
An example of paint being milled. The more times the paint goes through the milling process, the finer the pigment is ground. Milling also uniformly surrounds and bonds the pigment to the vehicle. Courtesy of Winsor & Newton.

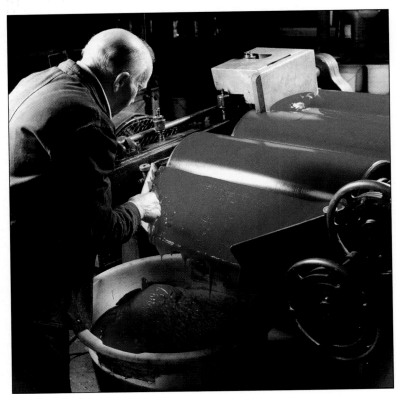

been milled three or more times to ensure that the pigment takes on the maximum amount of vehicle possible. In poorly milled oil paint, for instance, the oil may separate out and float to the top of the tube while the pigment settles to the bottom. If you have ever opened a tube of paint and instead of it having a nice thick toothpaste-like consistency the paint runs out of the tube as soon as the cap is removed, you have experience a poorly milled product.

The question then becomes: Is one paint really better than another? The answer varies. First, what is the intention of the artist? If you are a professional artist, you will want to spend the additional money to ensure the lasting quality of your creation, as well as the ease of application. As a student, the more reasonably priced paints will suffice and give good quality results. If it's a matter of being able to afford the lesser grade paint or not being able to paint at all, then the answer is to buy what you can afford. Artists such as Van Gogh and Picasso (when he was young) were more concerned with having paint and being able to express themselves than worrying about having the most expensive of materials to work with.

## Reading a Tube of Paint

There is a great deal of useful information on your tube or jar of paint if you take the time to read it. All tubes or jars of paint should list the type of vehicle used, and the pigment and lightfastness rating (Figures 5-5a and 5b). These are key elements the artist or designer must understand. The pigment listing should be specific and show the chemical class and color index number. The color index is an international system for identifying colorants. The lightfastness rating will tell you the color's resistance to fading or changing color when it is exposed to daylight. Colors that are not colorfast and are affected by exposure to sunlight are

**Figures 5-5a and 5b.**
A tube of Winsor & Newton cadmium red paint. Reading the tube of paint can give you important information, including the name of the hue and series or quality level of the paint.

The flattened label of a tube of Winsor & Newton cadmium red paint. The label also provides information on the exact pigments and vehicles used, as well as information on the permanence and lightfastness of the paint.

known as **fugitive colors.** All tubes and jars of paint should also have the weight or size clearly marked. This will usually be in both ounces and the metric equivalent. The last item that virtually all paints sold today have is a seal by the Art and Creative Materials Institute certifying that they meet all standard health requirements.

**Figure 5-6a.**
An example of the variety of different brush sizes within one brush tip shape. The number on the brush corresponds to its size; the larger the number, the bigger the brush.

**Figure 5-6b.**
A person attaching the hairs of a brush to the ferrule. The best brushes are handmade and hand trimmed.

Other items may also be indicated on a tube or jar of paint. These depend upon the manufacturer and type of paint. They can include the type of finish—ranging from gloss, satin, or matte—and are most normally found on acrylic or water-based media. Permanence, which is different from lightfastness, may also be indicated. This relates to the archivability of the paint or how long will it actually last. Professional series paints have a longer life than student or hobbyist paints. Some acrylic will also have the viscosity of the paint listed; this tells the user how thick the paint will be when it comes directly out of the tube or jar. Naturally, jar paints tend to be more viscous than tube paint.

## Brushes

There are three parts to any brush: the hair, ferrule, and handle (Figures 5-6a and 6b). Probably the least important is the handle. As long as it is made out of a good strong wood, there is very little difference among them. Some companies are now producing ergonomic handles that conform to the shape of the hand. One thing to check is if the handle is drying out or has any thin hairline cracks. This may mean that it is old and drying out and my not hold up well or last very long.

The ferrule is the metal barrel of the brush. The best ones are seamless and made from brass or copper, which will not rust. The hair is the key element. The type of hair used will make a great difference in your work. The finest hairs are Kolinsky red sable from Russia. They hold a sharp pointed tip and are very resilient. Weasel is a good and less expensive alternative. Squirrel is another alternative, but has much less "snap" to it. It is considered a good choice for working with very liquid paints, inks, or dyes. Camel hair is a manufacturers' trade name for squirrel, horse, or even goat hair. No, there's no actual camel hair—it's too coarse. The name merely refers to the color of the bristles or hairs. Synthetic brushes are getting better every year as new artificial materials are developed and may be a reasonable choice for the beginning student painter who may be cost conscious.

## More about Paints and Pigments

There are other factors or characteristics to consider when selecting colors. The masstone is how that specific hue of paint looks in a thick layer (Figure 5-7). When applied thickly, the color is very solid, dense, and opaque. The undertone is how that same hue of paint would look in a very thin layer. When the paint is applied in a thin layer, the true characteristics of the color emerge and become visible. The same color can look quite different when applied in a heavy impasto or in a very thin layer or wash.

The transparency of a particular paint is usually not a matter of how much pigment there is, but is actually a physical characteristic of the colorant itself. Some pigments are more opaque or transparent than others.

There are three major types of paint: oils, acrylics, and watercolors. They are the most widely used mediums. That is not to say that there aren't a number of other possibilities, including tempera, encaustic, and interference colors. Each of them has its own unique properties, chemistry, and uses. In addition, each requires a different type of brush to aid in the application of the paint to paper, board, or canvas.

## Water-Based Paints

Water-based paints can be divided into two major groups: gouache and watercolors. While they are both water-based mediums (meaning they can be thinned with water), there are a few basic differences. As for their similarities, they both use the same vehicle—

**Figure 5-7.**
An example of the masstone and undertone of permanent alizarin crimson. The masstone is the way the paint looks when it is applied in a heavy thick manner. The undertone is when the paint is applied as thinly as possible, showing it at its most transparent point.

gum arabic, the best of which comes from the acacia tree. The most highly prized comes from one source of trees in Senegal. What makes gum arabic special is its ability to mix easily with water and be totally transparent. This clarity of the vehicle allows all of the true color of the pigment of the paint to show through.

One disadvantage to watercolors and gouache is the way they bond with paper. The vehicle and pigment actually seeps into and bonds with the paper surface, or tooth. Because of this, they cannot be scraped or wiped off if you make a mistake the same way oils or acrylics can.

Watercolors are transparent and work extremely well when you want to build up layers of color with thin washes of paint (Figure 5-8). They come in both tube and cake form and, as their name implies, they combine well with water and can be thinned more than any other type of paint.

Gouache is opaque and gives the artist nice solid, dense areas of color. They are super loaded with pigments, which also helps to give them their rich full color. They also contain either chalk or calcium carbonate that gives the paint a dull matte surface with absolutely no

**Figure 5-8.**
Joseph Raffael, *Return to the Beginning: In the Memory of Ginger,* 1981. Raffael created this painting by working the wet paint onto a wet surface known as the wet-on-wet method. You can see the medium spread out as it is absorbed into the paper. Watercolors can also be applied to a dry surface, which will cause it to stand up more on the paper and not seep in as readily. Artists prize watercolors because they can create rich transparent layers of color.

surface sheen. Most often used by designers and illustrators, gouache was preferred over all other mediums because of its matte finish. In the past (only about fifteen years ago in precomputer times), artworks had to be photographed with a stat camera to be used in any type of production such as posters, magazines, or book covers. The dull matte finish made lighting easier because the artist and photographers no longer had to worry about any glossy reflection from the surface of the media. Other mediums, such as oils or acrylics, have a glossy shiny surface, which creates reflections of the studio lights on the surface of the artwork. Another major factor in gouache is that it is self-leveling, which means that as it dries and sets, it flattens itself out to create a smooth even surface. This also makes it ideal for reproduction, because the artist does not have to worry about correctly lighting an uneven surface.

There are three types of paper you can use when you work with watercolors. Hot-pressed papers are actually run through heated rollers in the manufacturing process, which seals the pores of the paper. This creates a fine smooth finish, but adds to the overall cost of the paper. Cold-pressed paper has a rougher surface and does not have a smooth feel, which allows it to absorb more of the liquid medium. Rough paper is the most textured and is excellent for creating dramatic effects.

**Oils**

As stated previously, oil paints use linseed and other natural oils as their vehicle. Trina Nicklas uses thinned applications of oils to build up the surface and give her work a richly hued quality (Figure 5-9). To thin oils, turpentine or mineral spirits are used. Today, more people opt for a product called turpenoid that has the same thinning properties, but doesn't have the noxious smell of turpentine. In either case, both should be used in a well-ventilated space since they are highly flammable.

However, there is a new product on the market that was introduced a few years ago—water-soluble oil paints. This may sound like a misnomer, but they are true oil colors that have been specially developed to be thinned with water or mediums. They clean up very easily with just soap and water.

They can even be mixed with traditional oil paint on a 2:1 ratio: two parts water-based oil to one part traditional oil paint.

## Acrylics

Acrylic paints were developed in the 1940s and really came into their own as true artists' materials in the 1950s and 1960s. They use an acrylic polymer resin as their vehicle and can be thinned with water or mediums, depending upon the desired effect. With acrylics, as the water evaporates, the resin molecules line up in a string formation and chemically bond to each other, creating a hard permanent durable surface. One nice thing about acrylics is that they are very forgiving to the novice painter. If you make a mistake, simply let the paint dry and reapply the new color over it. Because the paint dries hard and permanent, there is no fear that the undercoat will interact or bleed into the next application of paint. Acrylics have a very shiny glossy surface, but this can be changed with the addition of a matte medium. Dan Namingha uses this glossy quality of the paint in his brightly colored paintings based on his Native American heritage (Figure 5-10).

**Figure 5-9.**
Trina Renee Nicklas, *Breaking Away*, 1998. Nicklas is able to build up a rich surface quality by applying several layers of oil paint in a technique known as glazing. This ability to work in layers of color is one reason why artists choose to work with oils. You can achieve a heavier, more opaque covering or layer of paint than is possible with watercolors.

## Inks and Printer Inks

Inks come in several different types including permanent inks used for drawing and special inks used for printing computer-generated images. In the 1890s, Winsor & Newton was among the first to start

**Figure 5-10.**
Dan Namingha, *Ceremonial Hawk Kachina*, 1991. Renowned Native American artist Namingha creates a vivid Kachina-like image in acrylics. The use of acrylics allows Namingha to obtain very bright vivid hues in his paintings. Acrylics also allow the artist to build up a thick impasto easily and quickly to create a wide variety of textures.

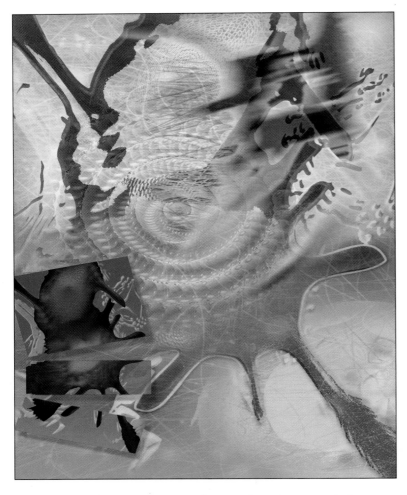

**Figure 5-11.**
John Labadie, *Hydrogen Alpha in Red,* 2000. Labadie is able to achieve a high degree of color in his digitally created works. In the past, the colors an artist could use for the standard printing process were limited. Today, artists are able to work with a wide range of color as evidenced in Labadie's work.

mass-producing inks. Inks are made from dyes mixed with a shellac binder that give inks their permanent water-resistant characteristics. Artists should take care when using inks since they are made from dyes and do not have the lightfast qualities of pigment-based products. White, black, silver, and gold inks are the exception, since they are made from pigments or metallics.

Printer inks for laser and inkjet printers come in four standard colors: yellow, cyan, magenta, and black. They can come preloaded in cartridges, and each one is especially designed for the make and model of the printer, or in a bottle used to refill your printer's cartridge. Artists can achieve a dynamic range of color with these new inks, as seen in John Labadie's work (Figure 5-11).

The biggest issue with these inks is their archivability. Most tend to be fugitive in nature and do not do well if exposed to direct sunlight for any length of time. Magenta is especially prone to fading. Most ink currently on the market has only a twenty-four- to twenty-six-year life span. This is very short life in terms of fine art, where permanence is highly valued. However, this is adequate for most design projects, which don't have the same life span. Still, the artist should be very careful not to unnecessarily expose the printed piece to sunlight and therefore increase the chance of the colors fading. Another important element in ensuring the archival life of computer-generated work is to use acid-free paper. Taking these steps will help prolong the life of your printed digital work.

## Colored Pencils and Pastels

Colored pencils combine pigment, wax, fats, oils, and other things that are shaped into thin tubes and then dried. The dried media is inserted into a wooden shield or frame for durability and ease of use. The wax binding used helps to resist and prevent the color from fading. Unfortunately, the wax can cause a problem called **wax bloom** in which a white hazy film develops over all or parts of the artwork. This problem can develop over time and is a result of the wax base rising to the surface and creating a snowy or milky look. One method to remove it is to take a soft tissue or cloth and very gently wipe it away. The bloom, which looks just like a flower, may return again in time. The only way to stop this is to apply a spray fixative to the work when you are finished. It may take several applications of fixative to seal the work completely.

Pastels as we know them today have been around for about the last 250 years, although artists have been using colored chalks for thousands of years. Since they are made from almost pure pigment with just enough binder to hold them together, they may be the purest form of colored media. The vast range of bright colors that an artist could achieve is what attracted many of the Impressionists to work with pastels. French artist Edgar Degas popularized the use of this medium in his drawings of ballet dancers. In the drawing in Figure 5-12, Degas used the intense color of the media to add a sense of atmosphere to the work. In addition, pastels allowed him to work quickly, capturing the gestures and movement of the dancers.

There are two kinds of pastels: oil-based and chalk pastels. The pigments employed to make pastels are the same that are used to manufacture oil paints. Chalk pastels can range from very soft to very hard, depending upon how much binder is used. The harder the pastel, the more binder and filler are used in its production. Today the most commonly used binder is methyl cellulose, which will not yellow or become susceptible to mold and mildew. The filler is usually clay or precipitated chalk, although many companies are using a mixture of aluminum, kaolin, and plaster.

Pastels got their name because when the pigment, binder, and filler are mixed together they form a paste. A stick of pastel is more correctly called a *pastellist*. Soft pastels with very little binder have much more brilliant

**Figure 5-12.**
Edgar Degas (1834-1917), *Four Ballerinas Resting between Scenes*, 1899. Pushkin Museum of Fine Arts, Moscow, Russia. Photo Credit: Scala/ Art Resource, New York, NY.
Degas elevated pastels to an accepted art medium. Prior to this time, they were only used as a sketching material. Notice the juxtaposition of the use of complementary hues, which add to the atmospheric quality of light produced in the drawing.

**Figure 5-13.**
An example of the color cast created by different light sources. All three were photographed using daylight film. The top image was photographed under fluorescent light. The center image was photographed using natural sunlight, and the final grouping was photographed using tungsten light. There is a dramatic color shift when the correct film and light source are not used together.

or just enough to hold the media together in a stick form. They also tend to be much larger in diameter than pastels. However, they use the same pigments as oil paint, as well as a small amount of inert oil and wax as binding agents. Because of this unique type of binder, they never really dry the same way oil paints do. While they may harden somewhat, they can stay workable for years and years. This is one reason all paintings and drawings created with oil pastels should be framed and covered with either Plexiglas or glass.

**Color Film**

Color film consists of three light-sensitive layers of emulsion held on to a film base. Each layer responds to one-third of the colors in the spectrum. One layer is sensitive to blue, another to green, and the other to red using the additive color system to achieve a full spectrum or range of hues.

There are a wide variety of color films on the market. They fall into two basics groups: color print film and reversal or slide film. Reversal films usually have the word "chrome" as part of their product name, such as Ektachrome or Fugichrome. After it is decided whether to shoot slides or negatives, the next categories or groupings of film are daylight and tungsten. Film is color-balanced to work in either daylight (sunlight) or under tungsten (regular incandescent lamps), according to their exact temperature based on the Kelvin (K) scale. Sunlight on a clear bright day would measure about 12,000 K or higher, while on the other hand, tungsten light measures in at only about 3,200 K.

Sunlight is much bluer than the light given off by standard light bulbs, which tends to have a warmer reddish cast. Most people tend to ignore the color shift and don't even notice the differences. Daylight films are color-balanced to obtain the most natural-

colors, but they tend to crumble and wear away very rapidly. Brightness is determined by the amount of chalk employed, which will also make the media more or less opaque depending upon the amount used. To achieve a full range of shades, black may be added to the pigment mixture.

Hard pastels and pastel pencils are much more durable, but they are less vibrant in color. The choice is between intense color or long-lasting durability, though many artists use a combination of both types in their work.

Oil pastels are also known as nondusting or dust-free pastels. They are not the same thing as oil sticks, which are oil paints combined with a very tiny amount of binder, looking hues when shot during the day with sunlight as the main source of illumination. They will also work well with most blue-based or cooler light sources. Color negative film is more tolerant of differing light sources than slide or reversal film. This color balance is less critical with new print films such as Kodak's Gold series. They are formulated to work in a much wider temperature range to allow the photographer a greater number of lighting options. Unfortunately, fluorescent light will not match either type of film and will give off a greenish cast (Figure 5-13). This can be compensated for by using a special fluorescent filter and by opening up the lens to one full f-stop. Daylight films are better suited for this purpose than tungsten because they are color-balanced to accept the bluer, cooler color range.

## Tattoos

One of the oldest forms of color application is tattooing, which is practiced on nearly every continent, with the possible exception of Antarctica. Many tribal groups from New Zealand to Africa to the Americas and Asia have all practiced this ancient art, including this form of body decoration as an integral part of their culture. In most cultures, tattooing marks a rite of passage usually associated with initiation into manhood or womanhood at puberty. It marks the individual's changing status within the group and moving on from being a child to an adult member of the tribe or group. It is a permanent application of color meant to mark the wearer for life. Psychologically speaking, in today's culture, it represents a person taking control and ownership over his or her own body, making a personal visual statement (Figure 5-14). Tattooing has become more popular in recent years. In a study in the late 1980s, only about 10 percent of people had tattoos, while a recent study by the University of Connecticut of

**Figure 5-14.**
Tattoos are a way for people to take control of their own bodies by making a visual statement about themselves and their ideas for all to see.

adults age 18 to 29 found that 35 percent of women and 30 percent of men now sported body art.

Tattooing is quite literally art by puncture. Ink or dye is placed (or injected) into the dermis layer of the skin by means of a hollow needle filled with pigment. Ancient tribal groups used bones and thorns by tapping them into the skin to place the color in a desired location. Today, a mechanical device rapidly vibrates a hollow needle that injects the pigment to the proper depth into the skin. In fact, most tattoo inks are not inks in the traditional sense, but can best be described as a pigment suspended in a carrier solution. The carrier has two functions: to place the pigment in a free-flowing aqueous concentration for ease of application and to act as a disinfectant. The first pigments were carbon black and other ground minerals. Today most pigments used are metal salts and the occasional vegetable dye.

### Sand Painting

Cultures as diverse as the Navajo and Nepalese Tibetan monks use colored sand as an art medium. One of the chief elements of all sand painting is its impermanence. It is temporal in nature and not meant to last for a great period of time. Their creators purposely destroy them as part of the ritual religious art-making and healing process. Finally, the sand is returned to the earth from which it came and the cycle is completed.

In Tibet, the art is called *du-ltson-kyil-khor*, meaning mandala of colored powers. The mandala, also know as a cosmogram, has a multitude of meanings on many different levels and has both an inner and outer meaning. The inner level represents a map where the human mind may be transformed into an enlightened one, and the outer level represents the world in its divine state. The sand painting is a vehicle for reconsecrating the earth and all of its inhabitants. Normal iconography can include geometric shapes as well as spiritual symbols. A single painting may take days, weeks, or even months to complete. Early mandalas used ground rubies for red and lapis lazuli for blue and so on, while today they are commonly made out of dyed sand. When complete, the sand is swept up and taken to a nearby river or waterway to return the sand to its natural environment and spread the healing energies throughout the world.

Navajo sand painting is used and created as part of healing ceremonies, also called Sings or Ways (Figure 5-15). These rites include prayers, sweat lodges, and medical herbology, as well as the construction of a sand painting. For the Navajo, the world must always be in balance or "hozho," and if this delicate equilibrium is upset, illness or some other disaster will result. To return the wold to harmony and beauty, a Singer (medicine man) leads a ceremony in which the sand painting is constructed. These events can last from one to nine days. *Iikaah*, the Navajo word for sand painting, means "a place where Holy People come and go," because they believe that figures created and represented are actually present during the ceremony.

**Figure 5-15.**
Navajo Man Sand Painting, circa 1990-2002, Arizona, USA. Sand paintings are created as part of healing ceremonies. After the ritual is completed, the sand painting is destroyed. The sand is applied by hand-spreading the colored grains between the thumb and forefinger.

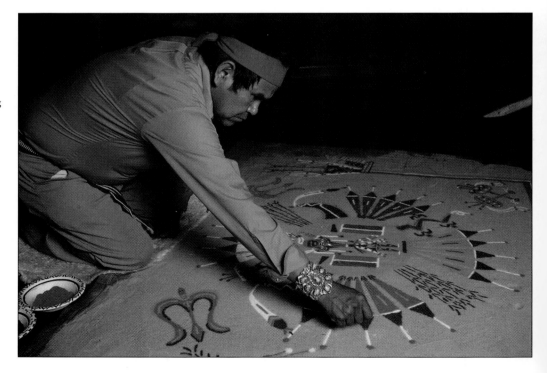

Since these paintings are so powerful, they cannot be created for any other purpose than that for which they were intended. Any painting seen at a gallery or museum is a re-creation with several important elements left out or removed. Only in this way can they be viewed by a secular audience because for many Native American tribes, there is no separation between life, art, and religion. They are one and the same thing.

There are approximately 500 different sand paintings derived from some 50 different chants or ways. For instance, there may be almost 100 different sand paintings within the Shooting Way or Shooting Chant. Each color has its own special meaning. For example, red represents sunlight. Only the sacred colors are used: black, white, yellow, red, and blue. They are linked to the four sacred mountains, as well as the directions of north, south, east, west, up, and down. These colored sands may be made from pollen or ground minerals.

A sand painting can be very small or quite large, measuring up to 20 feet. The Singer creates the images in the painting following a very strict prescribed format. There is no artistic license taken when creating a sand painting. If the images are not made correctly, it will not have any healing power. At the end of the ceremony, the patient literally sits in the middle of the creation while the Singer touches parts of the painting to the patient. Finally the painting is smeared out and obliterated. The sand is collected, placed in a blanket, and then taken away to ensure the health of the person treated.

In contemporary sand paintings, a board is sanded and smeared with a thin layer of glue. The sand or crushed stones are placed by hand and worked in, small areas at a time. The application of the glue must be precise. If it is too thick, the painting will be lumpy and messy, while if it is spread too

**Figure 5-16.**
Terry Achten, *Raku Jar with Lid*, 1996. The black matte color of the natural clay body creates a nice canvas for the glossy Raku glaze. Raku glazes use oxidation to bring out their unique colors.

thin, the sand may not adhere. These paintings are specifically created for a secular audience and are not imbued with the power of a healing work.

## Glazes

Glazes are used as a permanent coloring and sealant for ceramic ware. The glaze actually fuses into the clay during the firing process. A glaze is composed of three parts refractories that aid in viscosity, glass formers or silica, and a fluxing agent. Silicate, the substance which actually forms the glasslike surface, is also a component of clay and has a very high melting point over of 3,000 degrees Fahrenheit. This melting point can be greatly lowered with the addition of a flux agent such as lead, sodium, or potassium. Lead used to be a major component of most glazes, but has fallen out of use because of the fear of poisoning. It can leach out of a fired piece such as a mug or plate and be absorbed into the system of anyone who might use the ceramic piece.

At first glance, whether in dry powder form or mixed into a liquid, glazes look dull and drab and nowhere near the color they will be after firing. The high heat of firing is the key that unlocks the color. This is one reason why ceramists create test tiles of glaze to see what the final product will look like. A glaze can be matte, glossy, transparent, or opaque depending upon the minerals and pigments used, and they can be applied in several ways including brushing, dipping, pouring, and spraying. In Figure 5-16, Terry Achten uses both glossy and matte glazes in his Raku fired vessels. The black matte elements of the jar act as a framing device to show off the iridescent red and blue glazes.

Hobbyists and students usually learn by using commercially prepared glazes, which allow for ease of application and constancy in color and finish. The limiting factor is that the range of color available in commercially produced glazes is restricted. For these and other reasons, experienced ceramic artists often prefer to formulate their own glazes. Personalized glaze formulations are known as recipes. Each formula is measured out to very specific and rigid standards. A slight variation in the amount of any ingredient used could result in a drastically different finish.

The temperature during firing is also another factor that can change the final look of a piece. Therefore, glazes could be considered color created by using extreme heat to cause a thermal reaction. Just as with paint, ceramic artists use glazes to show their unique, personal color voice and vision.

## Summary

As we have seen, color can be worked within a variety of wet and dry media, each having its own specific use. In this chapter, we have reviewed most of the standard materials and the pigments that artists and designers use. We have even explored artworks, such as tattooing and sand painting, which are important because of their cultural or religious meaning. Pigments are the elements in the medium that give it its hue and color. The same type of pigment can be used with different vehicles to create a variety of different mediums.

Understanding which pigments and other elements are in the medium being used and how they have been processed enables the artist and designer to make appropriate choices when selecting a media for a project. The right media can make the piece. It is critical to know what the medium you are using is composed of to facilitate its use and archivability. The latter tends to be more important to fine artists whose original works should last for years to come. Designers are not usually as concerned with this because all of their work will end up in a digital format for commercial production.

All of the colorants and media reviewed in this chapter are part of what is known as the subtractive color mixing process. All pigments, paints, and inks are included in this general grouping. In the next chapter, we will discuss the additive process, or working with light, which is the basis for digital color.

## Digital Color: Chapter 6

If color is the most elusive and complex of all of the elements of design, then digital color is the most ephemeral of all of the aspects of color. In one sense, it doesn't exist as a solid material entity. While you can touch pigment—the dry powders that make up color within paint—a digital color element is pure light and has no tangible physical manifestation. Digital colors can only be seen through a monitor or as a printed piece. The actual digital creation is nothing more than a string of computer code, existing only within a software program such as Photoshop or Illustrator. It has no physical being except for maybe the space the code takes up on a CD, disk, or hard drive.

So when working with digital color, we are really dealing with a number of things:

- the computer code that creates the color,
- the output devices, such as the monitor or printer, and
- the picture element of pure light.

Digital color has seeped into all aspects of our lives. From the personal computer to every magazine or newspaper we read, from CDs and DVDs to the digital camera we bring with us on vacation, all are inexorably tied to digital color. Less than twenty years ago, few businesses and virtually no households had computers in them. Digital art was an interesting oddity that few people, including artists, took seriously. Now the digital revolution has come and gone, and computers are an intrinsic part of our daily lives.

There are many variables when working with digital color. Your monitor, scanner, printer, and the individual software program used can all affect the color perceived and produced. It is learning to control these elements in much the same way artists and designers have learned to control traditional color that makes all the difference in creating good digital creations. In my view, one is not inherently better or worse than another. Each has its place in the artists'

**Figure 6-1.**
An illustration showing each individual pixel that makes up an image. Notice that the pixels are actually squares of color similar to a mosaic.

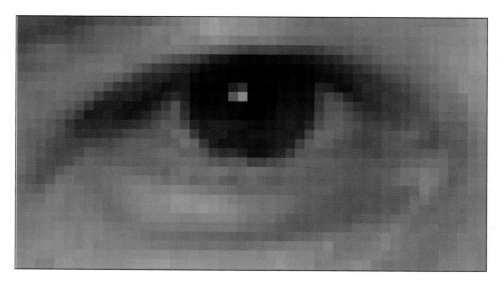

repertoire. It is really a matter of intention, selecting the right tool for the right job, that will most easily let you express what you want to communicate.

## Pixels

The most basic component of digital color is the **pixel,** a combination of the words *picture* and *element.* Composed only of light, pixels are two-dimensional and have only height and length but no width. They are flat square-shaped bits of light having no specific size (Figure 6-1). Their size is determined by their function and use.

Pixels are lined up in rows called **rasters.** Rows and rows of rasters make up the actual image. The amount of these elements in a one-inch space is known as the **resolution.** You may also hear it referred to as either ppi or dpi, pixels per inch or dots per inch. The more pixels per inch, the finer the detail that can be displayed in an image and the larger the file size. For example, an 8 x 10-inch image at 72 dpi will be a little more than one megabyte. A 300 dpi image of the same size would be more than 24 megabytes. In the digital world of color, size matters.

Different size resolutions are used for different things. A Web page is displayed at 72 dpi. The smaller file size allows for data to be sent quickly and more efficiently. A standard printed page from your favorite magazine is created at 300 dpi. This has to do with the way things are printed and will be discussed in more detail later on in this chapter. Line art such as contour line drawings or plans can be as high as 600 dpi. Here the more dots per inch, the finer and more fluid the line will be. If you have ever noticed that when looking at an image you see the stair-step effect on some lines or images, it's as if you are actually seeing the edges of the individual pixels themselves. These are known as jaggies or **aliasing.** Any time you see an anti-aliasing feature in a pixel- or

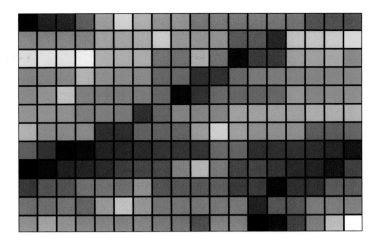

raster-based program such as Photoshop, check the box to turn it on. This will help to alleviate the situation and create a cleaner, more fluid line with no jagged or rough edges.

## Color and Pixel Depth

To understand color depth, it is important to understand how the hardware and software operate. The smallest unit of information is a bit. It can be designated as on or off or a 0 or 1. Bits are the basis for binary code or information systems, which are at the heart of all computer applications. Very early monitors used a one-bit system, which means that they are either on and illuminated, or off. These were the primitive one-color monitors of early computing, used primarily for data entry.

Eight-bit color can display up to 256 different colors (Figure 6-2). This is the standard Internet color space. While it is limited in its color range, it provides for fast upload and download time, which is critical in Internet applications. No one wants to wait for a page to load. The longer your page takes to come up on screen, the more likely the viewer is to quit out and move on to another site.

Twenty-four-bit color will allow the viewer 16 million different colors. This is the color range of your monitor, which

**Figure 6-2.**
Color swatches showing the 256 Web-safe colors. (Courtesy of Adobe Systems, Inc.)

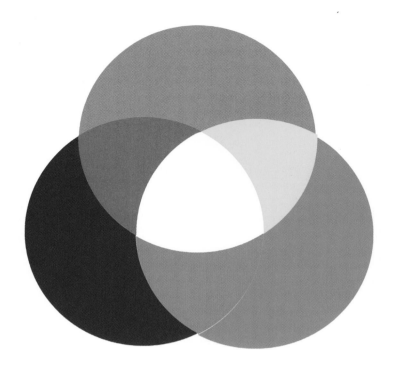

**Figure 6-3.**
Red, green, and blue are the primary hues in an additive color wheel. These hues are composed of light and not pigment, as in the standard primaries of blue, yellow, and red. Notice that in this system, blue and red make magenta, red and green make yellow, green and blue make cyan, and mixing all three primaries creates white.

**Vector-based programs** such as Illustrator, FreeHand, and Flash are not made up of pixels but are created using a mathematical algorithm or formula. Every time you drag the mouse and make an image larger or smaller, the computer recalculates the algorithm and creates the new image. Because they are not composed of pixels, the designs created can be resized at will without any loss of image quality, which makes them ideal for use in working with type or logo design.

## Additive Color

Previously, we were primarily concerned with subtractive color, which means that as light hits an object of varying or different hues, the wavelengths are subtracted or removed and what we see is what remains—the reflected color. When working with digital color, we are dealing with **additive color** or light itself. The primaries change from red, yellow, and blue (RYB) to red, green, and blue (RGB), as seen in Figure 6-3. Only when we print a picture will we again deal with subtractive color and even then the primary system will change from RYB to cyan, magenta, yellow, and black (CMYK).

## Color Pickers

There are several ways to pick color digitally. Just as in the traditional world, where there are watercolors, acrylics, and oils with their own unique properties, the digital world also has several color choices, or color spaces, to choose from. And again, just as with traditional colors, it is a matter of picking the right color space for the right job.

Color picking can be divided into two parts: the actual mechanical method for selecting a particular hue, and the overall color space. Each manufacturer has developed its own color selection devices. Adobe, Apple, and Macromedia all have their own proprietary color-picking

explains why your monitor can display a wider range of color than you can print or use on the Internet. Many modern games are now using this color space with its wider range of hues to create more realistic imagery and game elements.

## Raster Versus Vector

Not every computer program uses rasters. There are two major types of computer programs, raster and vector. Raster-based programs such as Photoshop are made up of pixels, and the image quality can vary with the amount of pixels or dpi in an image. They are also known as resolution-dependent programs, which means that image quality is based on the amount of dots per inch in a given image. Again, the higher the resolution, the better the quality and more detail contained in the picture. The images created can be made smaller, but they cannot be resized and made larger. This is because the computer program algorithm would have to add pixels to create the new information and the picture would become fuzzy or blurry.

apparatus (Figure 6-4). The one thing they all have in common is that they are based on a color solid or a three-dimensional color model. When we select a hue, we are taking a slice through that color space, selecting a specific point containing the hue, value, and saturation.

So whether they are arranged in a circle, sphere, or cube, the end result is the same. The four most standard color spaces or **color modes** to choose from are RGB, LAB, HSB (also occasionally referred to as HSV), and CMYK. Additional color modes also include grayscale, duotone, and a few others that are less frequently used. Choosing a mode is determined by the end use of the digital file or image. Most often artists and designers work in RGB and then convert the file over to one of the other modes when their work is completed. One reason for this is that you are working in the same color space as your monitor and many of the filters and other elements within programs such as Photoshop have only been designed to work in that mode.

RGB may be the most versatile of the color modes. It is for Web page design, as well as the initial creations for video and print work. After the design or artwork is complete, the piece can be easily converted to another color space for final printing or rendering.

HSB stands for hue, saturation, and brightness, or value. In this color space the artist can pick out each element as they define a color to be used in a digital work.

LAB is primarily a device-oriented color space. L stands for luminance, while A and B represent the two color areas within the mode.

CMYK stands for the four primary colors used in printing digital designs and artworks. Those primary hues are cyan (a medium blue), magenta, yellow, and black. Black is used to give depth and body to the images that are created with the other three colors.

The human eye sees a wide array of colors, giving it a very large color space. Computers cannot match the scope and breadth of the eye for the range of color it can reproduce. Color spaces are the defined areas or amounts of color that can be seen and reproduced accurately by a computer. Many of these spaces are created and set up for specific software or hardware. Figure 6-5 shows the differences in several color spaces, including the human eye, LAB color, and Adobe RGB 1998. The largest color space by far is the human eye, which can discern the widest range of color. Just slightly behind the eye would be LAB color, and the Adobe color space is even smaller.

**Figure 6-4.**
An example of the Adobe color picker from Photoshop. The large square is a slice of the solid color space. The spectrum at the right side of the cube is where the user selects the desired hue. On the right side of the dialog box are the various color spaces that can be selected. They include RGB, HSB, and LAB. Notice that CMYK cannot be selected—the values are only displayed for informational purposes. (Courtesy of Adobe Systems, Inc.)

**Figure 6-5.**
An illustration of the various color spaces. The size of the space determines how many hues can be distinguished. The larger the color space, the wider the range of hues that can be expressed.

Finally, the smallest color space is that of the Internet.

### Types of Computer-Imaging Programs

There are several different types of computer-imaging programs each designed for a specific use. There are vector-based drawing programs, which excel at line art and more graphic uses such as logo and package design. Raster-based programs are designed to work with continuous-tone images such as photographs or painted images. Going hand in hand with these programs are the digital layout programs including QuarkXPress and InDesign. These are prepress programs developed to replace the traditional page layout.

### Monitors

Your monitor can have a dramatic affect on color. Such variables as the type, age, and condition of the equipment can radically alter the color displayed. Monitors fall into

a few specific types: either cathode-ray tube, liquid crystal display (LCD), or plasma screens. The vast majority of monitors used in homes, schools, and industry is the standard cathode-ray tube model. It works in much the same way as your color television set does with the main difference being that your TV has a receiver, channel selector, and antenna or cable hookup. But the picture screen works in exactly the same manner.

The age of your monitor also plays an important role in the amount of true color that is visible. The average life span for a monitor to show accurate color is only about three years. If you want to see this for yourself, stand in a computer lab and look at all of the monitors. You will notice that each monitor may have a slightly different cast to it. This may mean that either the monitors may require calibration or that they are very old. As your monitor ages, the phosphors in the tube weaken and cannot display a full range of hues. In addition, as

**Figure 6-6.**
A diagram of the inside of a traditional cathode-ray tube monitor showing the screen of phosphor dots. The three electron guns—red, green, and blue—fire through a shadow mask and stimulate the phosphor dots that create the image on the screen.

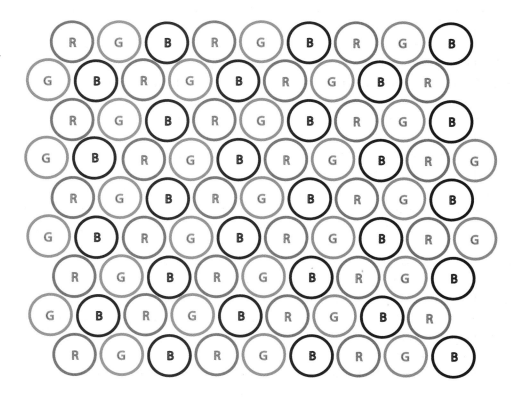

your monitor ages, it must be calibrated much more often.

## Gamma and the Monitor

Monitors use an additive color mixing system (RGB) to produce color. It emits red, green, and blue light in the varying proportions required to show a specific hue. As an example, yellow is made up by combining red and green. Since there is no blue present, the computer assigns it a value of zero. A bright yellow might be assigned the following values: red–241, green–244, and blue–0. To see for yourself, open a computer program such as Photoshop or Illustrator, go to the color picker, and plug in these values to see the actual nature of yellow hue that is displayed.

The traditional cathode-ray tube monitor screen (Figure 6-6) is covered with phosphor dots or stripes arranged in sets of three, called *triads*. An electron gun fires its beam of electrons through a shadow mask, stimulating the three phosphors in each triad. The glowing of these specks or stripes in the triad is controlled by the current of the electron beam. Since the phosphors are grouped closely and tightly packed together, they are viewed as a single pixel or dot of color. As a monitor ages, the phosphors dim and hence change the color that is displayed. As mentioned earlier, this is one reason why older monitors need to be calibrated more frequently than new ones. When an image is displayed on the screen, the color of each pixel is determined by the color values in the image file or color profile. A television set works in the same way as a computer monitor; however, the main difference is that the TV also has a receiver to change and control the selection of stations and programs. In North America, a television picture on screen is composed of thirty pictures per second flashing on the screen, while in Europe it's only twenty-five pictures per second.

**Gamma** is the measurement and mathematical formula of the relationship of voltage input to the relative brightness of the image seen on the screen. It is measured on a scale, or range, of 1.0 to 3.0. If the gamma is not set correctly or if your computer's operating software doesn't automatically correct for it, the colors and their related values seen on screen will be dramatically affected. Personal computers (PCs) and Unix systems usually run a 2.5 gamma and usually require gamma correction. Macintosh and Silicon Graphics platforms operate at a normal gamma of 1.8. They do not have to be corrected because the graphics card in the Mac automatically corrects the gamma, and the hardware of the SG machine performs the same function. For PC users, upgrading to Windows 2000 may be helpful.

## Describing Color: Gamut

Each hardware component used to create color images or pages reproduces a varying range of color, or gamut. **Gamut** is the actual range of color each device can display or reproduce. Monitors, scanners, printers, and presses each have their own gamut. Within each manufacturer, the gamut for a product can vary. If one manufacturer makes several different monitors, as most do, each one may have a different color gamut. Also, gamut ranges change from device to device. For example, you can see a wider range of colors on screen than you may be able to print with your printer. Your monitor and scanner use different color models and describe their colors differently than your desktop printer or a commercial press. You may have already noticed that the colors you see on your monitor and the colors of the final printed image can greatly vary. This is why we calibrate a monitor to the exact make and model of the printer and even the paper that will be used.

## Color Management Modules

The gamut of all color output devices from monitors to printers is far less than the range that can be seen by the human eye. To try to correct this situation as much as possible, each piece of hardware uses a **color management profile**. This profile is tagged or assigned to each file as you save it. Have you ever noticed that sometimes when you open a file, you get a warning dialog box that tells you there is a profile mismatch between the manner in which the file was created and the setting on your machine? It then asks you what you want to do about it. Your choices are usually to correct it in one of two ways or to discard the color profile completely.

You never want to discard the profile and throw it out. Your two choices are to either assign it a profile that matches the machine you are working on, or to use the imbedded profile in which the document was created. If you know how the file was created, you may decide to keep the imbedded profile and if you're not sure, then you may want to go with the working profile of the computer on which you are working. If you are on your home computer, you probably have set up your computer with the correct profiles. However, if you are working in a lab situation, either at school or at a commercial printer like Kinko's or any other commercial printing house, check the settings on the computer before you actually change your file. You never know who was sitting at the computer before you and what their level of knowledge was. Never assume anything. Remember, it's your artwork at stake.

## ICC Profiles

Part of the color management model is an ICC profile, which is a standardized formula or format developed by the International Color Consortium (see Chapter 2, Color Theory: Making Sense of Color). These formats describe and explain the attributes and behaviors of color devices such as printers, scanners, and monitors (Figure 6-7). They were developed to be used by all manufacturers as a way of standardizing color. Each device has its own profile and is based upon a table of key reference colors. This table of colors is standardized by device to ensure uniformity between all related hardware platforms. For example, a monitor will have a reference table of the red, green, and blue phosphors that are used in that monitor. Since different manufacturers use different phosphors, individual tables need to be developed for each monitor.

Therefore, the most accurate means of color management is to have each file created with the tag of that device that includes its ICC profile. This in turn allows every other device to read the tag, interpret the data, and display the most accurate rendition of the colors used in creating the document.

**Figure 6-7.**
An illustration of how the color management models and device profiles work together to translate the color space from one device to another.
(Courtesy of Adobe Systems, Inc.)

## Color Calibration

The only way to ensure that what you see on your monitor and what your printer will produce are similar is to calibrate the monitor. Calibrating sets up the ICC profile so that other devices, such as your printer, can read it and deliver accurate color. Depending upon the age and type of monitor, you will have to determine how often this function must be performed. The older the monitor, the more frequently this procedure will have to be done.

## Input Devices

There are several types of input devices or ways to bring an image or artwork into your computer. Scanners, digital cameras, and storage devices of varying shapes, sizes, and styles will all allow you to bring in an image or design. You can even create one from scratch using a painting or drawing program. Keyboards can also be considered input devices since they can add and change data, but they do not bring in or import visual data, which is what we as artists and designers are primarily concerned with. Understanding how your input devices work is equally as important as understanding your output devices. They are both key in creating digital artworks; otherwise, what we would be left with is a series of unreadable ones and zeros locked away within the computer itself.

## Scanning

By far, scanning is the most widely used way of bringing in or importing an image into the computer. Flatbed, film, and drum scanners are most frequently used in image creation. As with everything else in the digital world, each has its own specific function and use. By far the most widely used are flatbed scanners. The top lid lifts open much like a Xerox or copier, and a document or image is placed face down on the glass top. It works by shining a bright beam of light that moves down across the entire length of the image. The light is calibrated to the brightness of sunlight for true and accurate color reproduction.

Perhaps you have noticed that when using a scanner, there are two steps the machine goes through before it begins scanning your original. The first step is to calibrate the equipment and the second step is to warm the lamp. Warming the lamp is important for several reasons. First, if the lamp stayed on constantly, it would burn out on a regular basis. It would also become so hot that it would either melt the plastic casing or it would have to be made out of metal to stand the heat produced by the bulb. Users would be forced to wear asbestos gloves to prevent skin burns. In the warming process, the lamp heats up to the correct temperature (measured at about 55,000 degrees on the Kelvin scale) and brightness for accurate color reproduction.

The second step in the scanning process, following the light source, is the CCD chip or charge-coupled device (Figure 6-8). This is what actually scans in your image. It reads the light energy given off by the light

**Figure 6-8.**
A scientific CCD chip with broadband spectral response manufactured at MPI Halbleiterlabor. A CCD chip reads light energy. It is the heart of your scanner or digital camera. (Photograph courtesy of MPI-HLL/Filser).

reflecting off the original on the platen glass. These readings are translated into a digital format by the scanning TWAIN program and either processed into an image in the native scanning program or translated into a software package, such as Photoshop. TWAIN, which actually stands for "technology without an interesting name,"or **twain acquire,** is the technology used in the scanning process. The programmers who developed the scanning protocol inside Photoshop could not come up with a suitable name for this new feature and left it with its working moniker of TWAIN.

Most digital cameras also use a CCD chip to capture an image and then store it on a reusable card such as a compact flash or smart media card. These cards can either be reused or a new card can be installed as the working card becomes full with images. Digital cameras are rated using the concept of megapixels. The amount of megapixels a camera can take will determine not only its price, but also the maximum output size an image can be printed at while still retaining highest optimal resolution. As a rule of thumb, the least expensive cameras, such as 2 and 3 MP (megapixel) cameras, can only produce photographic quality pictures no larger than about 5 x 7-inches; 4 MP is about 8 x 10-inches; 5 MP is about 11 x 14-inches; and so on.

### Web Color

By far the smallest color range is Web color. With only 256 distinct hues, the artist and designer are limited in creative color use. Speed in downloading a Web page is one of the primary concerns of most Web designers. If a page takes too long to come up on screen, a viewer may get bored and move on long before the image can be displayed. So file sizes must be kept small to speed up the launching time. In this mix, something has to give and one thing is

color. New software packages have made it easier to work with Web color by creating special color-picking devices that only display Web-safe hues. These eliminate the guesswork regarding whether a color can be displayed properly. In addition, there are special file formats used in Web page design. The JPG/JPEG (Joint Photographer Expert Group) format, was developed to work with continuous-tone images and creates smooth photographic Web images. CompuServe GIF (graphic interchange format, the full formal name), is more commonly shorted to GIF and is a good file format for solid color and very simple gradient elements such as backgrounds, banners, and buttons. Another advantage is that GIF files are very small and download quickly.

### Online Versus Printing

One of the newest file formats is SVG, or scalable vector graphics. They allow the designer to download a graphic from the Web and then directly use it in a vector-based drawing program. As yet there is no such equivalent in the continuous-tone or raster-based world. These types of images cannot be downloaded and printed with any real image quality. Again, resolution is the key factor: a Web image is at 72 dpi and a true professional-quality image for the print world is created at 300 dpi. An image downloaded from the Web and printed will look **pixelated**, which means that you can actually see each individual pixel that makes up the image. These images look grainy and have a very poor quality. So as yet, these two separate worlds (the Web and the printer or printing press) are never to be as one. Even if you were going to reduce the resolution as far as you could at 150 dpi and still print an image off a home printer, the difference in resolution may still be great enough to be visible to the naked eye.

## Printing

When printing an image from a computer, you are going from the additive process of the monitor to a subtractive process of printing using inks. Most printers use a four-color ink printing process or CMYK, which stands for cyan, magenta, yellow, and black. Black, which is represented by the letter K, actually stands for the term *key* and is used to add richness and depth or value to the print. As stated previously, you cannot print the full range of colors seen on your monitor. One of the other differences between the monitor and your printed output is that the printed work will appear darker than the screen version. You have to remember that the image on screen is very bright and backlit and is more similar to a transparency than a print or photograph. Its color is more saturated and brighter on screen than your print will be. In addition, things print darker in value than when they are displayed on a monitor. The artist or designer must learn to compensate for these elements when preparing to print a document or image.

Another key factor to remember when printing is that each printer and brand of ink used will produce slightly different colors in your image. When an artist or designer needs to match a color exactly as in the packaging of a product or in a logo, they use what is known as a spot color. The most commonly used spot color system is the PANTONE brand color-matching system. PANTONE offers a wide variety of color and paper stocks to choose from. Most color-picking devices have a separate selection screen or pop-up menu for these colors, as well as a few other color-matching systems (Figure 6-9).

Exact color matching is important because consumers reach for an item based on its color. We have been trained and conditioned to unconsciously react and respond to a specific product's color. But if you're skeptical, just think of the following: What color is the

label on a Campbell's soup can? What color is a can of Sprite? What color is the McDonald's logo?

### Inkjet, Laser, and Giclée Printers

There are many different types of printers on the market today. The vast majority of home printers are inkjet. They offer the widest range of use at the cheapest price. This doesn't mean that they are inferior in quality. Like anything else, you get what you pay for. However, there is a wide range of excellent inkjet printers on the market made by Epson, as well as a number of other companies. Many design professionals use these in their studios for proofing, making comps for clients, and creating fine art prints.

Inkjet printers usually use liquid ink, while laser printers use a dry powder toner. Another interesting note is that for many printing jobs, users do not have to change their images from RGB to CMYK to print out a single copy of an image. The CMYK format is normally used only when printing a large production run, and the file is converted to CMYK only after all of the work is complete and it is ready to go to the printer.

The high end of inkjet printing is the giclée print, also known as Iris prints. The name is derived from the French verb *gicler* meaning to squirt, or more accurately in this case, an

**Figure 6-9.**
The Adobe color picker using the custom color setting for PANTONE colors. There are several different types of PANTONE colors to choose from, including coated to uncoated and metallic finishes. (Courtesy of Adobe Systems Inc.)

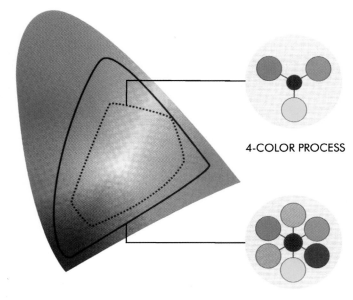

4-COLOR PROCESS

7-COLOR PROCESS

**Figure 6-10.**
A diagram of the ICC color profile showing the traditional four-color space and the new seven-color space. Notice how much larger the new space is. This means a greater variety of color can be produced and printed without the addition of spot colors. (Courtesy of Adobe Systems, Inc.)

extremely fine spray of ink. The application of the inks in this printing process is so fine that there are no discernible dots or droplets of ink on the final print. Many fine artists use this process to produce a limited number of print sets and high-quality reproductions.

Laser printers are ultra high-resolution printers. A heat process melts toner powders onto the paper. These printers are used for either single image printing, limited runs, or editions of a print. But for high-volume printing such as magazines, books, and posters, a press is always used.

### PostScript

**PostScript** is a page description language developed by Adobe initially for the Macintosh. It tells the printer specifically how to create and print an image on a page. Over the years it has become the gold standard for desktop publishing and printing. At the time PostScript was developed, Microsoft's software developers were busy concentrating on business-based applications and let the graphics market fall by the wayside. This is one of the reasons why most graphic designers

or people who are concerned with the printed image tend to be Mac enthusiasts.

### Raster Image Processor (RIP)

A RIP or **raster image processor** works hand in hand with the PostScript language and actually interprets the data or code, translating the instructions. A RIP is built into most desktop printers, but it is a separate module for imagesetters.

### Dot Gain

One of the many variables in printing is the porosity of the paper and the spread of the ink. These variables are known as dot gain. The rougher the paper's surface or tooth, the more the ink will bleed or spread as it is applied to the paper's surface. On the other hand, if the surface of the paper is smooth, the ink may bead up and only spread out a tiny amount. This flow of the ink onto a particular paper can be compensated for and set up in the application or printing programs. For example, in a program such as Photoshop, the flow of ink is adjusted or set up in the Color Settings menu application.

### Production Printing

Production or commercial printing is normally done for large runs of prints, from several hundred to several thousand. Most presses also use a standard four-color printing process (CMYK), but they can also be loaded with special inks for a wider range of color and exact matching of color that is not normally available in other printing processes. These special colored inks are called spot colors. They can be PANTONE, Trumatch, or Focoltone inks. The newest form of production printing is high-fidelity color printing. Instead of four inks, additional colors—including orange, violet, and green—are added. This allows for a larger color space, as seen in Figure 6-10.

## Four-Color Separations: Plates

To print on a commercial press, each image or page of images must be divided into four parts, one for each of the four colors of ink (Figure 6-11). These are called **separations**. In the past, these separations were produced photographically and created by means of colored filters. Today they are created digitally and stored as files. Normally there are only four separations created unless spot colors are also used. In this case, a separation must be made for each spot color as well. A halftone screen or plate is created for each of the separations. Each plate will be loaded with ink and used to print the piece, as seen in Figure 6-12. Computer-to-plate imagesetters are also used to create printed pieces. These are also sometimes referred to as direct-to-plate imagesetters. This process eliminates some of the steps in the printing process and thereby saves printing costs.

## Video and Video Cameras

Today there are two types of video cameras. Traditional analog video cameras use magnetic tape to capture the image. Digital cameras use a CCD chip, the same capture device as a scanner. It captures the light hitting it and converts it into electrical impulses. Currently most cameras use 1/4- or 1/3-inch chips that contain 270,000 to 680,000 pixels. Unfortunately, this is still under one megapixel, while most still-format digital cameras are now using 4- to 5-megapixel chips. So why go digital over analog? Digital videos can be copied easily and these copies are as clear and sharp as the original. They have CD-quality audio. But most of all, they use component color sampling which retains three times as much color information as analog video and gives the user more intense and accurate color reproduction.

The newest entrants into the software market are digital video editing programs. They can be as simple as I-Movie, which can

**Figure 6-11.**
An example of the CMYK separations. Each of the four channels will be made into screens for the production printing of the artwork or design. (Separations courtesy of David Bleicher.)

**Figure 6-12.**
This final printed piece, the face of a postcard, was used as an invitation to a gallery opening for a solo exhibition of my work in 1992 in Washington, D.C.

**Figure 6-13.**
Scene from *The Game Room*, Exodus Entertainment. Notice the detail and fullness of the figure. The animators are able to achieve a great variety of textures through careful lighting and attention to the effects of light on color.

be learned in a matter of hours (and comes preloaded in new Macintosh computers) or as complex as Adobe Premiere or Final Cut Pro, which are professional-level software packages. They enable artists and designers to create, edit, and produce movies, commercials, and even their own music videos. This is revolutionizing the industry because now designers or design teams can create their entire production in-house and not only save money, but also retain complete artistic control over the product.

## Animation

Animation used to be a laborious process where individual cells were drawn, inked, and painted by hand. Thousands and thousands of these were then photographed one by one to create an animated movie. This process was expensive and may have in part lead to the decline of animated productions in the 1970s and 1980s. In the 1990s as computers began to dominate still art in the design fields, new software programs were

developed to create animated or moving images. The 1990s saw a resurgence in cartoon or character animation with such Disney hits as *The Little Mermaid* and *The Lion King*. While most of these movies were still produced using traditional animation techniques, the filmmakers began adding elements that were digitally created, as in the stampede scene in *The Lion King*.

Most digital animation software programs are vector based. They allow the user to set up a virtual two- or three-dimensional space depending upon the program's capabilities. This fabricated space is where the action will take place. Programs such as Flash are 2-D programs that are used in all aspects of design. Flash is also one of the primary programs for creating animation on the Web. Three-dimensional animation programs including Maya, Softimage, and 3-D Studio Max allow filmmakers to create convincing dimensional characters and spaces, as seen in a scene from *The Game Room* (Figure 6-13).

Most 3-D programs use a **wireframe** model that is covered with a **texture map**. Figure 6-14 shows a wireframe, which is like a digital armature. It is a structure on which the animator can apply a skin that consists of texture and color information. The texture map contains information on the simulated textures and their corresponding colors (Figure 6-15). The other basic element in these programs is the lighting component. The 3-D programs use light and light direction or camera angles to integrate their relationship to color. It is important for animators to understand the effect of light (and lighting) on color. Poor color and lighting management creates flat characters. On television, if you watch many of the digitally animated shows that cater to very young audiences, you will find that the color tends to be overly bright and that the images appear a bit flat with a very shallow sense of space. This occurs when the lighting on the character or object is off. In many television productions, color form management is sacrificed in favor of economics. Time and money are key factors in producing these shows. Spending the necessary time to get the lighting correct is a luxury only permitted to the makers of feature-length animated films.

At the other extreme, companies such as Pixar invest heavily into developing accurate and correct lighting and color management. They will even develop their own software algorithms to create the desired visual effect. One of the first totally digitally animated features was *Toy Story*. Later releases such as *Monsters, Inc.* and *Finding Nemo* have raised the bar on digital animation. In fact, *Finding Nemo* is fast becoming the highest-grossing animated movie of all time. Digital animation is here to stay. In fact, it may not be long before actors in live-action films could be replaced by virtual counterparts, as alluded to in the movie *S1m0ne,* in which Al Pacino plays a director who creates a virtual leading lady.

**Figure 6-14.**
Brett Baker, 3-D Studio Max.
An example of a wireframe model. Notice how not only the ball and shoes each have their own wireframe armatures, but the space they exist in also has its own wireframe structure.

**Figure 6-15.**
Brett Baker, 3-D Studio Max.
The same scene as in Figure 6-14, but with the color and texture map laid over the wireframe model. Baker uses image-based lighting to create the naturalistic illumination and color for the elements.

**Figure 6-16.**
An example of a scene colored and lit using a radiance map. (Radiance map images courtesy of Christian Bauer.)

**Figure 6-17.**
The same scene as in Figure 6-16, now showing what it would look like at night. The advantage of this type of lighting is that the scene can be changed from day to night (and everything in between). without reshooting or additional editing. (Radiance map images courtesy of Christian Bauer.)

on a given surface. The information is then modified using the hue, saturation, and value adjustment. The images in Figure 6-16 and Figure 6-17 show the same scene reflected on a highly polished sphere. The sphere acts to distort the light and take in more of the image or scene, similar to using a wide-angle lens. Even under these complex conditions, the color and lighting in the cityscape scene are convincingly re-created. Using this new technique, digital animators can create more realistic color and lighting. After all of the sequences are shot and mapped, they must be compiled to produce the video or film.

### Safe Color Rendering

To create the final output, the digital files must be **rendered**. This is the process by which the computer collects all of the data from the digital animation program, the lighting, effects, and specified camera angles, and compiles all of the information to videotape or film. When transferring a digital production to film or video, intensely saturated hues such as bright oranges and reds can get blown out. This means that they appear to expand or flash over the object. It may look as if the color is bleeding or being smeared off the image. The actual color of an object can also be changed in this transfer process, as seen in Figure 6-18. This can be avoided by picking less saturated colors.

Another method for avoiding this type of color shift is to use only the National Television System Committee (NTSC) safe colors in the initial production. NTSC sets the standards for all video that is broadcast in North America. All standard (analog) televisions in the United States can only display video that conforms to these standards, which were finalized long ago in 1953, before the advent of videotape. Today, since most TVs can only display NTSC standard colors, most videotape formats are also restricted to this color space as well.

One of the methods now being used in digital animation to develop correct color and lighting is **image-based lighting**. The process emulates how light reflects off an object and scatters over surfaces. This process is accomplished by taking several digital photographs of an object, ranging from extremely overexposed all the way through completely black and underexposed. These lighting samples are combined through a special algorithm into a **radiance map**. The radiance maps are then used as the actual light source for the image or scene. They are also used to predict the reaction of light falling on an object by creating the proper color relationship to the quality of light

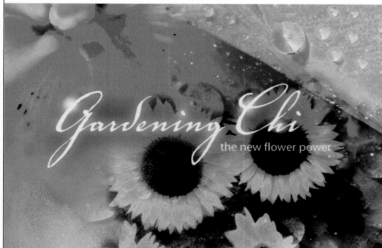

**Figure 6-18.**
An example of the difference between RGB and NTSC color spaces. The image on top uses RGB color, which has a much larger range of color than NTSC. In the bottom image, the color space was changed from RGB to NTSC and therefore simulates what would happen in the rendering process. Notice that the bright yellow in the upper-right corner of the top image is lost in the bottom one, and the color displayed is now a light yellow-green. In addition, in the center of the flower, the bright red-orange is too intense for the NTSC color space and is broken down into a few darker colors. What other differences can you find between the two images? (Courtesy of Adobe Systems, Inc.)

**Figure 6-19.**
An example of a gamut warning found in Premiere, a digital video program. The triangle with the exclamation point warns the user that the color selected is not an NTSC-safe color. If the user clicks on the little box below the warning symbol, the computer will select the next closest hue that can be reproduced properly. (Courtesy of Adobe Systems, Inc.)

Many animation software programs have an NTSC-safe color filter built into the program. Users should make sure the filter is enabled and turned on. When choosing colors for graphics such as titles or logos, the color picker of most digital video programs has a gamut warning (Figure 6-19). This is similar to the warning device found in print programs such as Photoshop or Illustrator. The difference is that in a digital video program, the warning is that the color picked is not an NTSC-safe color. The final method of testing for this type of color bleed is to view the production on a standard television monitor and not a computer monitor, which has a higher range of visible color.

**Summary**

Digital color is here to stay. Understanding it is as important to the fine artist as it is to the designer. Light is at the heart of digital technology. The artist or designer is now manipulating and mixing light to create color. The final product may stay on the screen or may be printed or transferred to film or video. Understanding how the transfer process takes place enables the artist greater control over the final product.

Today, there is no longer one primary color system. With digital color, the new primary systems of RGB and CMYK are added to the repertoire of artists and designers. Some people say that working with this new technology is more cerebral and less intuitive, but to the people who know how their hardware and software create and work with color, this method can be equally supple and expressive.

**7**

Up to this point, we have looked at color with an emphasis on two-dimensional art and design. The addition of the third dimension—depth—adds new complexities for working with color. No longer are we concerned about creating an illusion of space on a flat picture plane. We are now dealing with tangible space. There is a front, back, sides, bottom, and top to the object. It is real and exists in actual space.

All of the theories discussed previously still apply when creating art in the third dimension. Color harmonies are as important to the sculptor as they are to the painter, animator, or graphic designer. Every product purchased has been designed and great thought has been given to the color of that product. Toaster ovens, refrigerators, cars, and even toys are all three-dimensional objects designed to fulfill a need or desire. In many cases for the design of a product, extensive market research has been done to select the color of the item. Nothing is left to chance.

For the artist or sculptor, the choice of color may be more personal. Artists may choose a color to allow the piece to blend in or stand out. Sculptors understand that color can work like a magnet by drawing the viewer's eye to the piece. For all its

**Figure 7-1.**
Henry Moore,
*Reclining Figure*, 1936.
Reproduced by
permission of the Henry
Moore Foundation.
As light falls on the
sculpture, it creates
highlights and shadows
that feature the intricate
forms and add to the
feeling of depth.

importance in sculpture, color is normally ancillary to form. The overriding primary concern of the sculptor is the shape and articulation of the forms, with color being used as the chief supporting element.

There are special considerations when working in the third dimension with color. There are several choices that the artist must make before the piece is begun. Color can be derived from many different materials and applications. The material itself can have an intrinsic color, such as using stone, wood, or even metals. Color can be applied after the fact—the piece can be painted, stained, or patinaed. The color can be mixed into the medium when casting an object in plaster, plastics, or other material. But color is never an afterthought; it is an intrinsic element, and it can be a unifying element that brings the entire piece together.

### Value and Light

Since sculptures are three-dimensional objects, light plays an important role. The light falling on the object can create shadows in the crevices or undercuts by accentuating a specific part of the form. Value is also created on the body of the object by developing highlights in the parts closest to the light and shades of the original color in the portions farthest from the light source. As shown in Henry Moore's *Reclining Figure* (Figure 7-1), sculptors use these shadows to bring out important aspects of the volumes as they move in space. The large carved wood form of an abstracted female figure with its highly polished surface not only shows off the grain of the wood, but also creates a surface for the play of light. Two deep voids (holes that penetrate the sculpture) produce deep shadows and dark values. The light illuminates the planes of the figure, which can be easily seen in the highlighted areas at the side of the head, shoulder, and thighs, and brings out their form and mass.

### Innate Color

Innate or natural color is the color of the object itself. It could also be considered the local color of the object. Many artists who work in wood or stone choose a specific material because of its natural color and grain. Wood can range in color from birch, which is almost pure white, to ebony, which is a very dark brown nearly black in color. Stone, especially marble, can vary in color from white to green to pink and more, as seen in the examples in Figure 7-2. An artist will choose a specific type of stone or wood because of the color, as well as its ease of ability to carve and its permanence.

Looking at the gleaming white marbles of ancient Greek statuary, it is hard for us to believe they were once highly colored and decorated. Today, we see the unadulterated white stone as the purest and highest state of the art. For us, the white represents a classic beauty and purity. If someone were to paint these objects, there would be a loud cry that they were being desecrated. But in reality, they were painted with flesh tones to resemble

**Figure 7-2.**
These four examples begin to show the great variety of colors of stone that are available to sculptors and architects. Many artists choose a particular stone for its color. The lines running through the stone are called veins and are similar to the grain of wood.

**Figure 7-3.**
Constantin Brancusi,
*The Seal (stone)*, 1936.
© 2004 Artists Rights
Society (ARS), New
York/ADAGP, Paris.
Brancusi's concept of
truth in materials led
him to create sculptures
with highly polished
surfaces to bring out the
natural elegance of the
materials. He took great
care in selecting the
material for each piece
so that the color would
go hand in hand with the
forms he created.

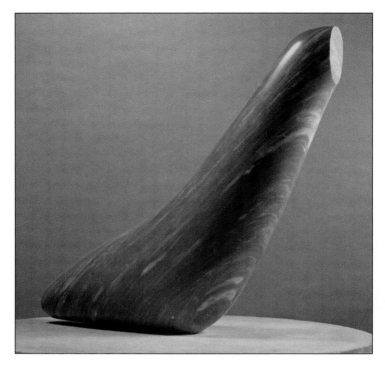

was at the heart of
Constantin Brancusi's
work. He espoused the
philosophy of **truth in
materials.** He felt that
sculptures should show
the natural beauty of the
material with which they
are created. Stone should
look like stone, wood
like wood, and so on.
Wood should not be
painted, and clay or
plaster should not be
patinaed (painted) to
make it look like another
material. The surfaces
should be finished off
in such a way as to bring
out the natural and

skin, and their garments were also highly
decorated and painted to add to their majesty
and opulence. It is only by today's standards
that we believe this concept is unthinkable.

Part of what led us to this belief is the pure
white marble statues of the Renaissance. The
sculptures of Michelangelo, with their highly
finished surfaces, have become our measuring
stick for sculptures from antiquity. What we
must remember is that by the time Michelangelo saw these earlier works, the paint had
worn away and he was laboring under the
same misconceptions and misinformation as
we often do. So he thought he was emulating
the past in the way he finished his sculptures.

### Truth in Materials

The concept of allowing the actual nature
and look of the materials to show through

innate qualities of the material. He believed
that artists should give great thought to what
material they were going to use before
starting a piece. The material and the
conceptual essence of the work must go
together and be thought of as one.

In *The Seal (stone)* (Figure 7-3),
Brancusi's streamlined forms and highly
polished surfaces became a hallmark of
modern sculpture. His concept was to find
the essence of the form and then to sand
and polish the materials to bring out their
natural beauty. He influenced the next
generation of sculptors, including Henry
Moore and Barbara Hepworth. Brancusi's
influence can still be seen today in the work
of Ursula von Rydingsvard, David Nash,
and many others.

### Stains

Artists will often search for a specific
piece of wood and try to find one with just
the right color and grain. Sanding and
polishing the final sculpture brings out the
inherent natural beauty of the material.

**Figure 7-4.**
Examples of the
treatment of a wood
finish. In the example on
the left, the bare wood
has been sanded smooth
to bring out the natural
grain of the basswood.
The center image shows
the same type of wood,
to which a clear coat of
polyurethane has been
applied. Notice that it
changes the color of the
wood and creates a
yellow cast. In the image
on the right, a walnut
polyurethane stain has
been applied. The wood
now has a deep rich
color that still allows the
grain to show through.

**Figure 7-5.**
Duane Hanson, *Janitor,* 1973.
Art © Estate of Duane Hanson/Licensed by VAGA,
New York, NY.
Hanson's figures have such a high degree of verisimilitude that people will come up and try to talk to the sculpture. Most of the people portrayed are the artist's friends and studio assistants. It was considered a great honor to be asked to be cast for one of Hanson's pieces.

### Applied Color

An artist has several choices when working with a particular media—either sand and finish the material, exposing the natural beauty of the material, or paint it. This leads us to another major philosophical outlook, which is to deny the intrinsic look of the media. In essence, the materials used—whether they are clay, wood, plastic, or metal—are nothing more than a structural entity used to create the artist's idea or concept. The material plays no importance in and of itself other than defining the form or forms of the sculpture. A material may be selected for ease of creation, weight, structural quality, or permanence. It can be painted or colored in any manner the artist desires to simulate a particular material, or it can be painted without any special concern to the original media.

One of the chief practitioners of this type of color usage was Duane Hanson. He painted his plastic resin cast figures to look as lifelike as possible. This method of working could be considered a form of *trompe l'oeil.* He worked from body casts of real people and then painted and dressed his figures to accurately resemble living beings. Hanson was part of the photorealist movement and his figures are so lifelike that people will actually stop and try to talk to them. Years ago when visiting the Milwaukee Museum of Art, I saw someone actually go up to Hanson's *Janitor* (Figure 7-5) and try to ask directions.

Artists often use the grain of wood or stone as linear elements within a sculpture. Stains can be applied to the wood after it is sanded to add additional color while still allowing the grain of the wood to show through (Figure 7-4). They may have a very distinct hue or be applied in a more natural, neutral shade to resemble the color of another wood, such as maple, oak, or walnut. They are painted on, rubbed in, and then wiped off to leave a thin coating that seeps into the wood. Varnish, shellac, or polyurethane is then applied to seal and protect the finish.

**Figure 7-6.**
Kenneth Armatige, *Richmond Oak*, 1985-86. Armatige creates a simplified metallic version of a real tree. The green patina is used to simulate the leaves and give them their characteristic color. Bronze is used and highly valued for its durability and permanence.

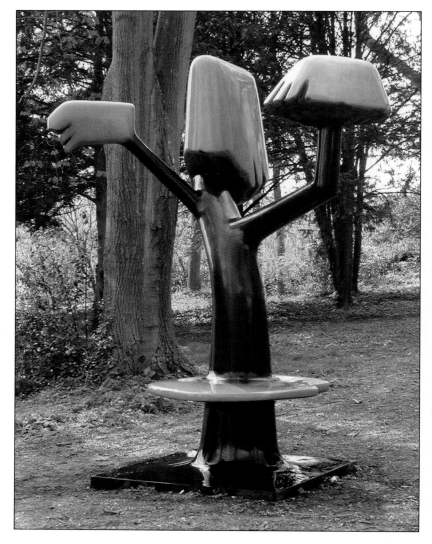

## To Paint or Not

Whether an artist decides to work with the natural color of the material or change it, it is purely an individual artistic choice. It is not a matter of right or wrong. Both are equally valid concepts when you are dealing with materials, whether you are building sculptures or anything else. These are some of the basic concepts that define the artist or designer and lie at the philosophical heart of the work.

## Paints, Colorants, and Patinas

Artists can use a variety of paints and colorants when creating a three-dimensional work. For coloring plaster, any water-based media, such as acrylics, and dry powder pigments can be mixed into the wet plaster. This is not a new technique—fresco paintings were created by mixing pigments into the wet plaster before applying it to a wall. Dyes can also be mixed into plastics before casting or direct fabrication.

Wood and metal are normally painted after the completion of the sculpture. Here the determining choice of paint may be made based on where the artwork will be shown or exhibited. If it is to be displayed indoors, a wider range of paints and colorants may be employed. If, on the other hand, the piece is to be exhibited outdoors, then acrylics or enamels must be used because they are impervious to the changing weather conditions.

Patinas are referred to when speaking about any coloring that is used to resemble and create the look of a weathered metal surface and are most often associated with plaster or ceramic sculpture. But true patinas are chemical agents used to color cast bronze and aluminum. These chemical solutions are most often used to oxidize copper, brass, and bronze, as well as ferrous metals, nickel, silver, zinc, and aluminum. Other chemical treatments include cupric nitrate, cobalt nitrate, and potash sulfurated (also known as liver of sulfur), which are primarily used on brass and bronze. In Kenneth Armatige's *Richmond Oak* (Figure 7-6), the green hue of the patina is used to mimic the color of leaves, as well as accentuate the form. The green patina also works to contrast with the dark color of the trunk and gives the sculpture a Pop art effect similar to a child's drawing.

## Clays and Glazes

We normally think of clay as ranging in color from red to brown. But the clay body itself can vary widely in color, due either to its natural color or by having minerals and oxides mixed in with it. This is most easily done while the clay is still in the dry powder form. White clay bodies can be mixed with cobalt to make blue, chromium for green, and carbon for black. The advantage to working in this manner is that the color is not just on the surface, but homogeneously mixed within the clay itself.

Between adding a colored clay body before modeling and applying a glaze after modeling, a stain can be used. Stains can allow for a wider range of hues and be more color stable than the oxides used in creating colored clay bodies. Another benefit to using stains is that their color tends to be brighter and more iridescent. As with creating colored clays, truer hues can be achieved when using a white clay body rather than using one containing iron oxides. Beth Ravitz paints and stains her clay sculptures (Figure 7-7), creating a blended surface. The look she achieves is more akin to the glazing method used in oil painting. She feels she is able to obtain a richer and more dynamic range of color using this method. She uses color to accentuate the modeled forms and to reinforce the underlying rhythmic structure of the sculpture.

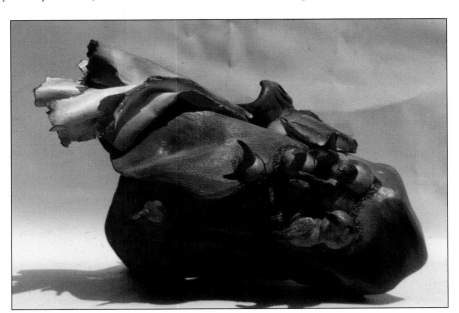

**Figure 7-7.**
Beth Ravitz, *Tetrial*, 2002. Ravitz uses paints and stains on her stoneware sculptures. She uses color to bring out and enhance the forms she creates and further the organic feel of the work. Ravitz uses cooler colors on the body of the piece and warmer hues to bring out the details on the surface.

**Figure 7-8.**
Dale Chihuly,
*Flori di Como*, 1998.
The Bellagio Hotel,
Las Vegas, Nevada.
In this piece, the ceiling
of the lobby of the
Bellagio Hotel, Chihuly
captures a variety of
vivid hues while working
with the transparency of
the glass. His work is
very theatrical in that
it uses swirling lines
and layers of color to
move the viewer's eye
throughout the ceiling.
Working with glass in
this manner is very labor
intensive. It takes several
assistants who work
closely with Chihuly to
create a glass sculpture
or an installation of
this magnitude.

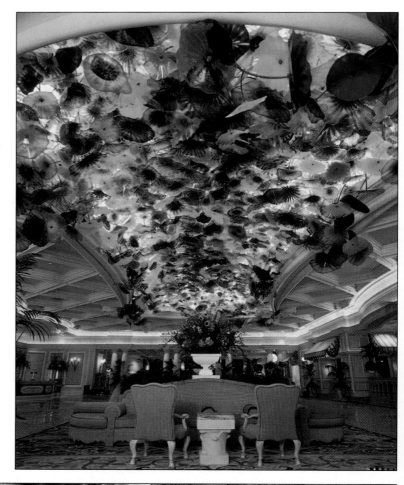

**Figure 7-9.**
Dale Chihuly, Detail of
*Flori di Como*, 1998.
The Bellagio Hotel,
Las Vegas, Nevada.
In this detail of the
ceiling, the transparent
nature of the glass
becomes more evident.
The shapes of the glass
forms Chihuly uses are
reminiscent of flowers,
shells, and other
organic forms.

Glazes are not only used in functional ceramics, but can also be used in ceramic sculpture. They are used in much the same manner as in creating utilitarian pieces. The added benefit to glazing a ceramic sculpture is that the glaze literally bonds with the clay in the firing process. This also seals the work and can make it invulnerable to the elements. One disadvantage of glazing is that a very large kiln may be required to fire a massive sculpture.

## Glass

The newest entrant to the arena of sculpture is glass. Artists such as Dale Chihuly (Figures 7-8 and 7-9) have rediscovered the beauty of working and shaping molten glass. Colored glass surfaces can range from transparent to completely opaque. Chihuly has a painterly approach to color and treats it in a fluid fashion. He is interested in the effect of light passing through the various layers of colored glass, which creates multilevels of transparency. Colorants usually in the form of metals or oxides are introduced into the glass in the molten state to create the wide array of hues used in glass objects and sculpture. In earlier times, gold was used as one of the metals used to create red, making it one of the highly prized and most expensive hues. Coloring glass in its liquid state can be tricky due to the high heat required and because it must cool very slowly to avoid cracking and shattering. Today, commercially prepared stains can be purchased to color glass. One of the drawbacks to using these colorants is that they are just painted on the surface and do not fuse with the material. This makes them susceptible to scratches and damage.

## Color and Dimensionality

Color can be used to enhance the three-dimensionality of an object and make the shapes appear more deeply cut into the form,

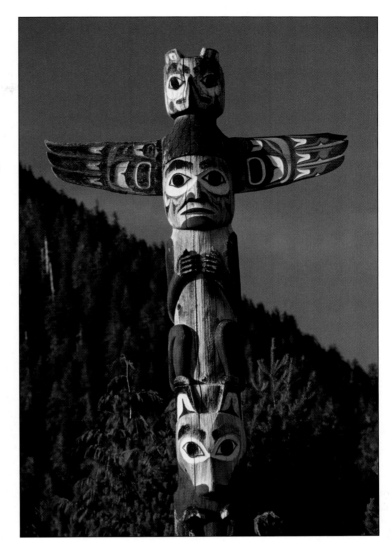

or it can be used to deny the dimensionality of the form and flatten it down.

The proper use of color can make the object or sculpture appear even more round and full of form than it actually may be. The Native American tribes of the Northwest Pacific coast were experts in their use of color to enhance the dimensionality of their sculptures. Totem poles or, as they are more correctly known, memorial poles are an archetypal art form of the tribes of the Pacific Northwest. These works are normally carved from large cedar poles with animal and other totemic figures stacked one on top of another. They are

**Figure 7-10.**
Detail of a Totem Pole, Saxman Totem Park, Saxman, Alaska.
© 2004 Clark James Mishler/AlaskaStock.com The figures on the totem pole tell the story of a great feat or event from tribal lore. The application of color on the planes of the form intensify the dimensionality of the piece which is actually carved in shallow relief. This can clearly be seen on the restored portion of the pole on the right.

**Figure 7-11.**
Frank Stella,
*Jarama II*, 1982.
The multicolored, highly
patterned surface of this
relief confuses the eye
and visually appears to
flatten out the piece.
This method of color
application is used to
deny the dimensionality
of the form. This begs
the question, At what
point does a painting
become a sculpture and
vice versa?

created and carved as one long, continuous piece and never constructed of separate sections. These forms may tell the story of an important event or tribal legend. Memorial poles (Figure 7-10) are carved in a very shallow fashion, almost in a low relief or three-quarter fashion since the backs of the poles are rarely carved or detailed. They are meant to be seen from the front or side. What gives them their sense of form and dimensionality is the application of color. Color is used to outline and define each individual form and make them more pronounced. The hues used may

vary between tribal groups and usually have specific meaning that relates to tribal lore and mythology.

Western artists have also used this concept to create contemporary sculptures. Jean Dubuffet created large sculptures out of cement and other materials. His childlike creations, which he dubbed "Art Brut," were meant to have a raw uncivilized feel as if they were untouched by traditional culture. Due to his use of color, they look more highly rounded than they really are. Each plane of the form either has its own color or is painted with lines going in different directions. By defining and showing off each plane, he gives a three-dimensional look to his sculptures, which were actually fairly flat with few if any undercuts. In this way, color creates form.

While using light to create value or painting each plane can bring out the dimensional look of the sculpture, color can also be used to flatten or negate the feeling of volume and mass. By painting or coloring an entire piece using very dark colors, the light falling on the sculpture cannot create visible shadows in the undercuts. This tends to flatten out the work and give it the appearance of a silhouette. The darker the hues used (including black), the flatter the forms will appear.

Another means of denying the dimensionality of the form is to paint the piece using vivid patterns and designs. Frank Stella used this method in creating *Jarama II* (Figure 7-11). The wild patterns create a visually confusing surface. Since the viewer cannot make out or discern the edge and contour of the form, it flattens out the mass, giving it an even look.

Over the years, three-dimensional form has come to include more than just traditional sculpture. It now has become the catchall for diverse things such as conceptual art, installations, performance art, and environmental works. In essence, anything that isn't two-dimensional or computer generated has been lumped into this category. Just as with traditional types of art, these newer forms also use color and each may have their own special considerations and color concerns.

## Conceptual Art

Conceptual art is a rather large area to cover and can encompass a wide range of art activities. It can take the form of written instructions or be comprised of photographs that document a previous activity, creation,

or event. It may be the most elusive of all the art styles to define or categorize. In conceptual art, the idea or concept is more important than producing a tangible lasting object. The act is the primal element, and it may be recorded in photographs or not, as desired by the artist.

But even conceptual art with its denial of the object and form uses color as an integral element. Most conceptual artists favor white as to be a noncolor and thereby severely limiting any cultural or psychological associations. In Yoko Ono's *Play it by Trust*, all of the pieces on a chessboard are painted white. After a few moves, it would become impossible for one player to tell his or her pieces from the other player.

In the late 1990s, blue bikes (Figure 7-12) began popping up all over Broward County in south Florida. Blue bikes were chained wherever one could conceivably lock a bicycle—from bike racks, to sign poles, and so on; blue bikes of all shapes and sizes magically appeared, one after another. Steve Sticht, the artist who created these **guerilla artworks**, came up with the color blue when he was working on construction, painting lines or stripes for handicapped parking

**Figure 7-12.**
Steve Sticht,
*Blue Bike*, 2002.
The blue color of the bikes makes them stand out and grabs the public's attention. The shade of blue is specially mixed for Sticht and has become his own "blue bike" hue.

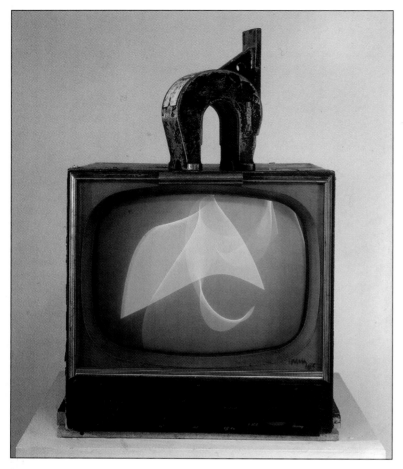

**Figure 7-13.**
Nam June Pike, *Magnet TV*, 1965. Courtesy of the Whitney Museum of Art, New York. Pike uses a magnet to alter the electromagnetic field of the picture tube, which creates the blue arcing lines on the picture tube.

reawakens a sense of wonder about one's environment. With more than 200 bikes placed within the area, the project is ongoing. However, many of them succumb to life in the city. Recently, one was totaled in a car accident in which a limousine jumped the curb, taking out a street sign with the bike attached to it. Still others have been stolen or dismantled and taken as souvenirs. The most recent additions now come with a sticker with Sticht's e-mail address to allow interested viewers to contact him for more information.

spaces. Sticht said the commercially prepared blue paint reminded him of the Day-Glo posters he had as a teenager. In the dark, the bright blue paint shined with an iridescent quality and allowed the bikes to be seen at night. Several years ago, the company changed the paint formula and altered its look, so Sticht had to bring in a sample and have the color matched. Now the bikes are all painted with what has become their own unique "blue bike" hue.

The bikes work on many levels. They are mundane items that would normally go unnoticed and be taken for granted. But the intense color forces the viewer to really look at the bikes and their surroundings and ponder the questions of why they were there, how they got there, and what their meaning was. Sticht believed this phenomenology

## Light Installations

Another kind of art that is hard to classify is the use of light. Whether it is the use of natural light or of lamps, these works tend to fall into the category of installations. This type of artwork can range from Dan Flavin's use of fluorescent lamps set up in a gallery or museum, to Walter de Maria's *Lightning Field*, a series of brightly polished steel poles placed in a grid in the New Mexico desert. The poles attract the discharge from lightning and create great arcs from the bolt to the pole that illuminate the sky.

A pioneer in the use of light and electronics, Nam June Pike created *Magnet TV* in 1965 (Figure 7-13). He was a founding member of the Fluxus group, a vague association of international artists. Their goal was to intermix art and commerce and create artworks that were both inexpensive and accessible. In this piece, the magnet interrupts the standard television signal and creates a series of vibrant blue dancing lines. The form the lines make constantly changes and moves, producing a form of kinetic sculpture or abstract television program.

## Landscape and Environmental Art

A number of artists today work directly in the landscape, both as the place and subject

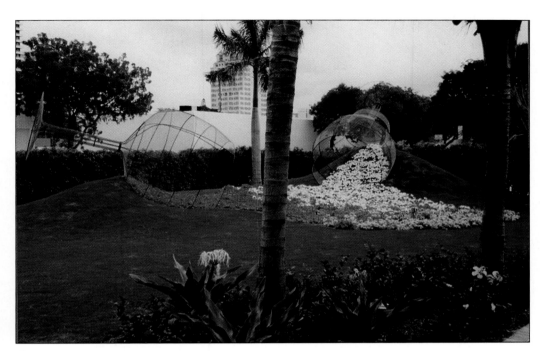

**Figure 7-14.**
Dennis Oppenheim, *Color Mix*, 1996. Image courtesy of the Artist, Photo: Tim Eaton Fine Art, West Palm Beach, Florida. Stretching out over a quarter of an acre, Oppenheim uses a mixture of red, white, and pink flowers to simulate the mixing of red and white wine. Unlike Goldsworthy's work, which is temporal and exists for a short period of time, Oppenheim creates a lasting work of art.

of their work. The landscape becomes both subject and material. One of the most notable landscape artists is Andy Goldsworthy. He creates large sculptures made solely out of elements found in the selected locations and never uses any additional elements such as adhesives, paints, or dyes. The colors in his works are from found leaves, rocks, or moss. All of the items used in his works are natural elements and come directly from the site of the piece. These works are also know as **site-specific** works, since they are developed for a specific location and actually become part of the environment. His work is ephemeral and impermanent. A photograph of the piece is the only lasting memento or record of the work.

Another artist who works with landscape is Dennis Oppenheim. Unlike Goldsworthy, he adapts existing elements or adds elements to the natural setting as required to suit the piece. The landscape merely becomes the setting for the sculpture. In *Color Mix* (Figure 7-14), Oppenheim planted red, white, and pink flowers to represent the liquid spilling from two wineglasses made of steel. As the colored flowers that represent the red and white wine pool together over the landscape, they create a middle ground of pink. Set against the blue South Florida sky, the warm hues of the flowers attract the viewer's eye.

## Performance and Body Art

Performance art is art that is acted out or presented in some manner or form. It may take place on the street, in a gallery or museum, or just about anywhere. Photographs or videotape may be made to document the event, but the act itself is the actual artwork. The art is in the doing. Both performance and body art arose, in some sense, in direct opposition to the highly intellectualized work of conceptual art. These works tended to be rawer and engaged the viewer in real time. They evolved from the feminist movement, in which a number of artists focused on issues of female identity and coming to terms with one's own body. Men were also influenced by these concepts of taking control and command over your

**Figure 7-15.**
Gina Pane, *Azione Psyche*, 1974. Photograph of a performance at the Galerie Stadler, Paris. In performance art, it is the act that is important. In Pane's work, it is not paint, but her own blood that gives the work its unique color. The photograph becomes the only record of the event.

own body. The art took on a sexual and graphic quality. The dangerous actions turned the viewer into a voyeur in a society where people had become immune to violence and bloodshed on television. These acts confronted the viewer with a harsh reality.

In Gina Pane's performance piece *Azione Psyche* (Figure 7-15), she cuts herself. The white color of her clothing creates a canvas and helps to make the red blood stand out and give it a more shocking graphic quality. It is also a poetic opposite—the purity of the white fabric against the dripping red blood. This is not a Hollywood special effect. These are powerful works because the viewer knows they are real, the blood is real, the pain on the person's face is real. And because of this, we have a visceral response to the work.

## Summary

Color is not just the domain of the two-dimensional artist or designer. It plays an equally important role in sculpture, industrial design, and all other forms of three-dimensional design. Color can also be used to make an object stand out and be noticed. The choice of material can dictate the color of the object. The artist can choose to bring out and enhance the natural color, grain, and texture of the media by sanding and polishing it to follow Brancusi's idea of truth in materials. Or the media can be painted over to form either a polychrome finish or a faux surface that simulates a wide variety of materials from stone to metal.

Color can be used to either enhance or deny the three-dimensionality of sculpture. Painting the various planes of an object with discrete areas of color will make the planes stand out and create a greater illusion of dimensionality, even in a shallow carving or relief.

Using wild patterns or designs can confuse the viewer's eye and flatten down the appearance of the object. The object can also be painted to mimic and blend into its surroundings, which is the basis of camouflage used by the military. With dimensional objects, the artist or designer is also dealing with the concept of value. As light hits the object, areas of highlights, middle tones, and shadows are created.

**Color and Fine Art: Chapter 8**

Color is an essential aspect of fine art. Whether it is painting, drawing, sculpture, or new forms of art, color is always a defining element. Even today's cutting-edge digital creations are concerned with the application and rendering of color.

There have been many art movements over the last 150 years, but the majority have been more concerned with imagery and subject matter than with color.

Color was relegated to a supportive or ancillary role. Only a few of these schools of thought have placed color at the fore-front of their philosophy. In this chapter, we will review some of the movements in art in which color played a major or dominant role in the underlying aesthetics of the artworks created.

It is interesting that something as powerful as color was not featured more prominently in more schools of thought. Color is one of the only elements in art that has an immediate unconscious response from the viewer's brain. As we have seen in previous chapters, people respond to color before they form conscious thoughts about what they are viewing. The first group of modern artists to understand the full impact of color was the Impressionists. The impact of light and its effects on color was the major focus of their work.

**Figure 8-1.**
Claude Monet, *Stacks of Wheat (End of Day, Autumn)*, 1890-91. Mr. and Mrs. Lewis Larned Coburn Memorial Collection, The Art Institute of Chicago. Monet used a warm palette of intense hues to create this painting of haystacks in the summer sun. He also placed complementary hues next to one another, which added to the luminous atmospheric quality of the painting.

## Impressionism

In some sense, contemporary art started with Impressionism. Our ideas of bohemian artists living in lofts or garrets and suffering for their art evolved from the myths and stories surrounding the artists of this time period. It may be the most overly romanticized time period in all of art history. But like all great stories, much of the tales are true.

Impressionism was a clear and dramatic break from the past and traditional academic painting. In everything from their use of color to the subject matter of their paintings, the Impressionists broke new ground. The effect of light and color was the primary focus of the group; however, each member concentrated on his or her own particular area of interest. Claude Monet focused on the great outdoors and even created his own gardens at Giverny. Edgar Degas became interested in the ballet, while Pierre Auguste Renoir had a lifelong fascination with the effects of light on the human figure.

The Impressionist's goal was to bathe the subject in light and paint the atmosphere to capture a moment in time. They were the first to understand and realize that as the time of day changed, so did the light and therefore the color. Monet and Renoir would bring several canvases with them when they painted outdoors. As the time of day and light changed, they would stop working on one canvas and begin another. This was a radical departure from the past when artists would bring one canvas with them and work on that painting all day long. They understood that in the morning the softer light would produce specific tints of color and that at noon when the sun was strongest, the color would be more intense and saturated with fewer shades. As the light of day began to fade in the late afternoon, more shades of a given hue would be used. Not only did the

**Figure 8-2.**
Claude Monet, *Stack of Wheat (Snow Effect, Overcast Day)*, 1890-91. Mr. and Mrs. Martin A. Ryerson Collection, The Art Institute of Chicago. Monet felt the color of the atmosphere (especially in winter) was violet. He used a cool palette composed of blues and violets and added its complement— the toned down orange color of the haystack. There are a few traces of pure hue used as highlights at the top of the haystack to create highlights and give the feeling of the winter sun.

light change throughout the day, but even the time of year would have an effect on the color. As the seasons changed, so did the quality and amount of light and color. Monet did several paintings of the same subject at different times of the year. These studies included the Rouen Cathedral, the Houses of Parliament during his extended stays in London, and the wheat stacks pictured in Figures 8-1 and 8-2.

The Impressionists also limited their use of black. They would only use it if the actual item they were painting was black, such as a man's shoes or a locomotive. But they planned out their pictures and subject matter to avoid these items. Instead of mixing black with a hue when creating a tone or shade, they would mix the complement of the color to darken and desaturate it. They would also add white to the complementary mixtures, which creates a warm or cool grayish color. This too was a departure from the traditional academic training of a painter.

In addition, they would juxtapose complementary hues to heighten the color in a painting. By placing two complements next to each other, they would cause a sensation in the viewer's eye, making the color appear more intense and vibrant. This added to the luminous atmospheric quality of their paintings.

In the traditional painting of this time period, the paint was laid down and applied in a very smooth manner. The objective was to hide the actual stroke of the brush and create a completely smooth surface. The Impressionists, however, applied their paint in short dabs or strokes, breaking up the surface. This also led to the pronouncement of the critics that their work was unfinished. In fact, the term *impressionism* was actually an insult hurled at the group by an art critic. The painting that sparked the debate, *Impression, Sunrise* by Claude Monet, was ridiculed saying that it was unfinished and merely a study, not a complete, finished work of art.

The Impressionists also wanted to paint contemporary life. They believed that they were living the ultimate in modernity and

**Figure 8-3.**
Katsushika Hokusai, *The Great Wave*, 1831. Victoria and Albert Museum. Flat areas of unmodulated color were dominant features of Japanese prints. The use of asymmetric compositions was another common element in these prints and greatly influenced the Impressionists' use of space in their compositions.

embraced the changes brought by the industrial revolution. They painted their friends and the places they frequented—the bars, cafés, and even the brothels. It would be as if today's young artists painted the bars, dance clubs, mosh pits, and even the malls where young people hang out. This concept of one's life being a worthy subject matter to paint was novel. With the rise of a burgeoning middle class, this change in subject matter had an audience, and this made their paintings more accessible to the general public.

During this time period, new artworks were beginning to enter the marketplace. Japanese prints (Figure 8-3) were being brought over from Asia, and their flat use of color influenced the group that came to be known as the Postimpressionists. The large off-centered groups of dancers found in Degas paintings and pastels are a spatial device gleaned from Japanese prints. Paul Gauguin and Vincent Van Gogh even painted versions of the prints they saw and collected. They were influenced by the use of broad areas of flat, unmodeled color and the sense of space. Gauguin's flat watered-down planes of color may also have been adapted from the styles seen in these prints.

## Pointillism

Pointillism is chiefly associated with Postimpressionism, as seen in *Sunday Afternoon on the Island of La Grande Jatte* by Georges Seurat. This painting, a study of which is shown in Figure 8-4, may be one of the most famous paintings of this style and period. Not only did it continue the themes of modern life, but it also broke new ground in its use of color and application of paint. Painting with small dots or dabs, Seurat took Rood's color concepts and applied them to

**Figure 8-4.**
Georges Pierre Seurat, *Study for A Sunday on La Grande Jatte*, 1885. The Metropolitan Museum of Art, bequest of Sam A. Lewisohn, 1951. Photography by Malcolm Varon. Photograph © 1984 The Metropolitan Museum of Art. Seurat did numerous full-size and small studies for this painting. Clearly illustrated in this study are the tiny dots or dabs that make up the painting and give it the stylistic name of pointillism. Seurat was one of the first artists to paint the frame and incorporate it into the work. At this time, most artists still framed their work in large gilt frames.

**Figure 8-5.**
Chuck Close,
*Elizabeth*, 1989.
(Courtesy of Pace
Wildenstein.)
Close uses photographs
as the basis of his
paintings. He transfers
to the canvas using
an underlying grid
structure. The highly
decorative surface of his
work keeps the viewer's
eye moving between the
colored dots that make
up the patterned surface
and the overall image.

painting. In visual color mixing, artists do
not premix their colors on a palette and then
apply them to the canvas, but instead they
paint tiny dots or points of pure unmixed
color. These hues, when placed next to each
other so that they literally touch one another,
blend in the eye or mind of the viewer. While
Seurat may receive the most recognition and
credit for developing this method of painting,
he was not the only one to paint in this
manner. French painters Camille Pissarro and
Alfred Sisley both took turns working with
this method of painting. Even Vincent Van
Gogh used a variation on this style in several
of his canvases. But instead of tiny dots of
paint, Van Gogh used longer brush strokes of
color, placing them one next to the other.
Since his application of paint was so thick
and heavy, where the two colors met they
sometimes actually blended, as one brush

stroke of wet paint touched the following
brushload of wet paint.

In the 1980s Chuck Close revived
elements of this style in his large-scale
portraits (Figure 8-5). While visually they
make reference to pointillism, his painting
process is more closely related to four-color
production printing, with one color placed
on top of another in a layered effect. In this
way, his work has an immediate relationship
to halftone and screenprinting, in which an
image is made up of tiny dots. He starts out
with a photograph of the sitter, enlarging it
to a monumental size. A grid is drawn over
the enlargement and a corresponding grid is
marked out on the large canvas. Close then
goes about painstakingly painting each cell,
building up the colors. He was never really
part of the photorealist movement; his
paintings don't share their same smooth
surface. But still, his work has an
unemotional surface treatment more
closely allied to minimalism.

### Fauvism

Brilliant color was at the heart of Fauvism.
This new movement grew out of the path
blazed by the Postimpressionists Paul
Gauguin, Vincent Van Gogh, and Pierre
Bonnard. Artists in both France and
Germany sought to liberate color. No longer
were they tied to local color; it could be used
purely as a means of expression. Events
could take place on the canvas that were not
tied to reality. André Derain painted red
boats on a yellow river with a violet bridge.
He used color for its emotional quality and
not as a representational element. Henri
Matisse began his career as a Fauve painter.
He felt color should be used in an expressive
manner. In Figure 8-6, Matisse paints
his wife in a free, bold style without
reference to natural hues. The subtitle of the
painting, "the green line," refers to the light
green line running down the center of the

woman's face. The line divides the face into two hemispheres: one on the left in harsh yellows and one on the right in a more natural tint of ochre. The background is simply flat planes of color used to fill out the composition. This new freedom of not being bound to the natural world helped pave the way for cubism and the move toward abstraction. The Fauvists broke away from all forms of naturalistic representation.

## Abstract Expressionism

Abstract expressionism and its descendant, color-field painting, seemed to be natural outgrowths of the cubist and surrealist movements. In these new styles, the imagery of the past was cast aside completely for pure of color paint. Taking its cues from automatic writing and Jungian philosophy, abstract expressionism sought to release the unconscious mind of artists and allowed them to create raw uncensored works. In the post-World War 2 era, these new movements were now becoming American art forms centered in New York in response to the past, in which Europe and especially Paris were the centers. Artists such as Jackson Pollack stepped away from the tube of paint and turned to the commercially produced can of paint. This is an important change for painting and color. No longer was color to be squeezed out of a tube of paint and mixed on a palette, but used straight from the can. It was felt that new forms of art need new materials—modern materials.

Color-field painting was directly concerned with the application of color to the canvas. In these works, the canvas was removed from the stiff formality of the stretcher and used as a space where the liquid events could take place. Paint became a vehicle for color—watered-down and at times used right out of the can. In both of these forms of painting, but most prominently in color-field painting, the

happy accident was promoted and became an elemental part of the work. The artist would set up a situation of how the paint might be thinned or poured, but the actual results were partially up to chance. The artist's hand, and most importantly, the brushstroke, was removed from the final artwork. In more contemporary interpretations of color-field painting, the primary interest is still color, but the artist's hand has returned, as seen in the gestural strokes in Janet Gold's work (Figure 8-7). Working in an almost triadic harmony, Gold creates richly textured layers of color using pastels.

## Minimalism

Minimalism was in sharp contrast and direct opposition to the more ephemeral and

**Figure 8-6.**
Henri Matisse, *Madame Matisse (the Green Line)*, 1905.
© 2004 Succession H. Matisse, Paris/Artists Rights Society (ARS), New York.
Statens Museum for Kunst, Copenhagen.
The left side of the face has warmer hues while the right side contains more cool colors. The violet eyebrow on the right side of the face is a complement to the dominant yellow used on the left. Matisse was highly regarded for his use of color and is considered one of the supreme colorists.

**Figure 8-7.**
Janet Gold, *Intimate Space*, 2002.
Gold uses pastels for the richness of their color. You can make out the individual strokes of the pastels as she builds up a complex layering of color. Her color scheme is primarily composed of secondary hues.

emotional aspects of abstract expressionism and color-field painting. The desire of artists Donald Judd and Carl Andre was to eliminate traditional spatial illusionism in favor of the pure plastic quality of the materials. The artist's hand and any trace of it—such as brushstrokes, imagery, or even the tactile surface quality of the material—was eliminated in favor of a pure streamlined, almost antiseptic, surface. Minimalism, as its name implied, sought to refine and reduce form down to its most basic element, allying it more closely with architecture of the international style. In this style, color was also pared down or even eliminated in favor of the natural color of the materials that echoed Brancusi's truth in materials. When

used, color was bright, saturated, and simple so that it would not take away from the form of the work itself or create any illusionist attributes.

**Op Art**

Op art, or optical art, was a movement that emerged during the same time period as minimalism. Both shared the use of simple flat unmodulated color. They also shared the complete absence of any evidence of the artist's hand to produce slick smooth surfaces. Op art used kinetic effects and optical illusions to create the feeling of movement in still flat surfaces. Victor Vasarely's *Kedzi* (Figure 8-8) appears to be a fully three-dimensional sculpture. It is,

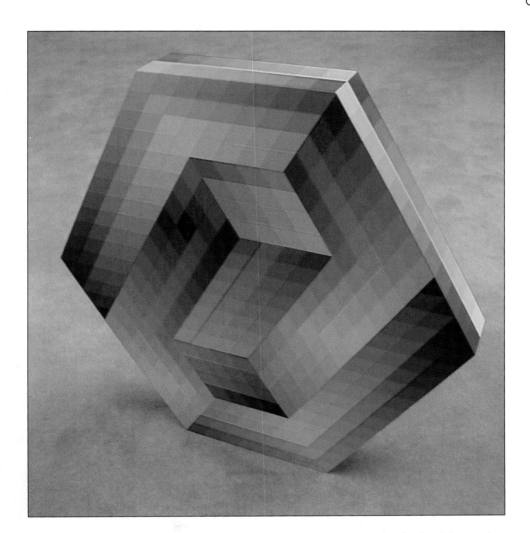

**Figure 8-8.**
Victor Vasarely, *Kedzi*, undated.
©2004 Artists Rights Society (ARS), New York/ADAGP, Paris. The sculpture, which appears to be fully three-dimensional, is really a flat plane. The 3-D effect is purely an illusion. The creation of illusions were a major factor in op art.

however, completely flat and only offers the viewer the illusion of dimension. The colors are shaded as if to suggest that light is hitting a perpendicular surface—a complete illusion.

Art, especially modern art, is constantly working in opposition and in contrast to what preceded it. As each new "–ism" or style emerges, it seems to be in direct contrast to what directly preceded it. The new photo-realists of the 1980s were a direct response to color-field painting, minimalism, and conceptual art. They returned to the human element and the craft of painting. One had to be quite skilled and able to paint in a photorealistic manner. This style returned realistic local color to the mainstream. Color had to be rendered correctly and accurately

to aid in the naturalist look of the work. The high degree of verisimilitude brought back issues of atmospheric perspective and shading as important for the artist. Their paintings also had the glossy look and surface of the photograph. Since these artists grew up with photography and television as seminal influences in their lives, it is only natural that they would be reflected in their artwork.

These artists were intrigued by the commercial landscape of the city, which became their primary subject matter. Unlike earlier movements, the natural pristine landscape is nowhere to be found. It is the city with all of its bright shiny consumerism that attracted the artists. In still-life painting

**Figure 8-9.**
Nancy Hagin, *Milk Glass Bouquet*, 1986. (Courtesy of Fischbach Gallery.)
Hagin presents the viewer with a wide variety of textures and surfaces. She uses a realistic naturalist color palette, and the color is slightly heightened. Hagin uses color in a traditional manner, with the warm colors bringing objects like the flower and ribbon to the front of the picture plane, and the cool colors receding in space to create a sense of depth.

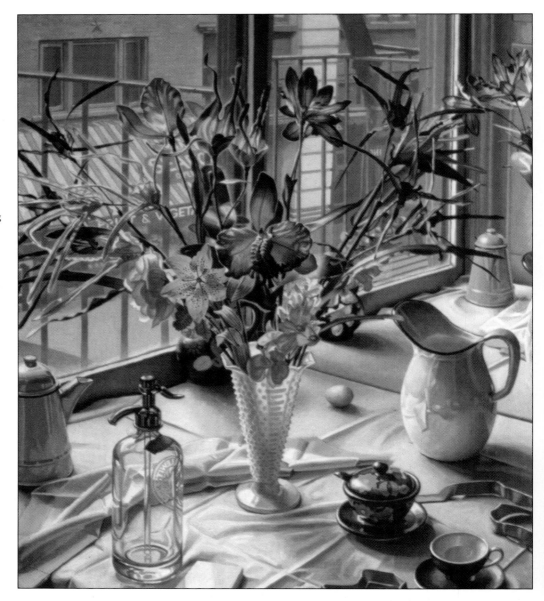

of this period, highly reflective surfaces such as mirrors and crystal dominated. These surfaces were hard to capture realistically and showed the virtuosity of the artist's skill. A prime example is Nancy Hagin's *Milk Glass Bouquet* (Figure 8-9), which contains a range of textures and surfaces from the soft petals of the flowers to the hard surfaces of the porcelain pitcher and glass siphon. Hagin renders each object with an exacting eye and captures their local color and value accurately.

## Neo-Expressionism

Arriving on the New York scene at about the same time as the photorealist movement, neo-Expressionism was primarily a European import most notably from Germany and Italy. This makes sense, since the earlier expressionist movements of the 1900s also had their start in southern Europe and Germany. It was yet another response against the established genres of minimalism and conceptual art. Sandro Chia was one of the leading proponents of this style to arrive on the New York art scene from Italy.

Chia uses color to elicit an emotional response from the viewer (Figure 8-10). Much of his work has a mythological basis to it. The male figure struggles under the weight of the large fish he is carrying. They both seem to have emerged from a brightly colored sea of colors. Placing the figure on a diagonal creates an underlying feeling of movement and heightens the sense of the man's struggle with the fish. The orange of the man's skin echoes the same hot hues found in the fish's tail and the background. The warm intense hues work in contrast to the cool blues creating a vibrant surface.

Americanized versions of this movement, led by Basquiat's graffiti style, have been linked to pop culture in the forms of rap and hip-hop. In both of these groups, however, there was a renewed belief in the power and possibility of painting. The neo-Expressionists' paintings were emotionally and physically charged. By using color as an important element, it gave the artists a more visceral component and enabled them to reach the viewer's subconscious by tapping an emotional wellspring.

## Aboriginal and Outsider Art

Issues of feminism, sexual identity, AIDS, and race came to the forefront during this time period. These were dynamic times where the art world was constantly in movement and flux. New interest in other forms of art also surfaced. Outsider art, including that of untrained or self-trained artists and the artwork of indigenous peoples, began to gain respect by the traditional art establishment.

In Darby Jampijinpa Ross's *Water and Emu Dreaming* (Figure 8-11), the colors used are reminiscent of the desert where he grew up, with its yellows and ochres. As with Navajo sand paintings, the true nature of the art

**Figure 8-10.**
Sandro Chia, *Water Bearer*, 1981.
© Sandro Chia/ Licensed by VAGA, New York, NY.
Chia regularly uses an intense atmospheric background in his work. Only the figures have the solidity of form created by the use of cooler colors and more solid areas of paint.

cannot be presented for secular viewing. Their art forms are sacred, and over the years versions have been adapted and developed for general audiences. Ross, like many other aboriginal artists, creates paintings like this one for a secular audience. On the most superficial level, the painting tells the story of the rain and the clouds it came from. It shows the path of the floods caused by the downpours. The two circles are their campfires and between them are the digging sticks that are used to find food. The dot patterns, which are typical of aboriginal art, represent the "dreamtime," which may be described as the relation and balance between the spiritual, natural, and moral components of the world. It is a time prior to living memory or experience—a time when creator ancestors and supernatural beings roamed the earth and sky.

The Yuendumu and Warlpiri use a full range of hues in their work, unlike many of the artists from other regions of Australia who prefer more traditional subdued palettes. They believe that the use of color should be celebrated. If you ask a Warlpiri

The colors used are
reminiscent of the
natural earth tones
that would have been
used in traditional
dreamtime paintings.
Brighter hues are now
incorporated into their
palette, including the
pinks and reds that
come from the use of
modern acrylic paints.
In paintings such as
this that are created
by men, the wavy
lines usually represent
ceremonial journeys.

artist about this, they will tell you that these
colors are everywhere and all around them.
These are the colors of the world—the blue
from the sky and the yellow from the sun.
Because of their love of color, they have
adopted the use of acrylic paints, which were
brought to them by a visiting anthropologist.
The new media affords them a wide variety
of intense hues with which to work.

The 1990s saw the boom and
commercialization of the personal computer.
Technology began to take a more dominant
role in art and culture, therefore reflecting its
importance in daily life. Computers were
everywhere—at work, in the home, and as
entertainment in the form of video games. It

was only natural that artists began to pick
up and experiment with it as an art tool.
Art and technology have always gone hand
in hand, and artists have been interested in
the technology of their day.

Auriea Harvey still considers herself a
sculptor. She says that all she has done is to
trade in her traditional tools for digital ones.
In *Entropy8Zuper!* (Figure 8-12), the Web
site she created with her partner, Michael
Samyn, they exhibit *Genesis, Exodus,* and
*Leviticus.* Their work has been influenced
by the movies in the widescreen format and
video games. In *Exodus,* viewers (or users as
they might be called) are offered the chance
to blow up airplanes. Their flat, unmodeled

**Figure 8-12.**
Auriea Harvey and
Michael Samyn,
*Eden Garden*, 2001.
A scene from
*Genesis* located at
www.entropy8zuper.org.

**Figure 8-13.**
Debbie Rose Myers,
*Judgement Day*, 2001.
Myers uses an intense
field of bright yellow
as the dominant color,
and balances it off with a
deep blue in the sky. The
yellow light is not naturalistic looking, but a harsh
hue. Hints of orange work
in contrast to the blue,
which feels more like that
of a nighttime sky.

images work well within the limited color space of the Web.

The use of the computer and other digital technologies includes both two-dimensional and three-dimensional creations. Some artists have worked in a purely digital world with their art remaining on the computer and viewed only via a monitor or projected onto a screen. Others use the medium as a creative tool and print out the final work on everything from paper and canvas to acetate. Debbie Rose Myers creates her photomontages on the computer and then has them printed on canvas (Figure 8-13). Using the computer, she can add or change any specific hue to suit her work without regard to its natural color. The bright intense palette she uses reflects her south Florida roots. This is a natural occurrence since artists tend to work with colors that influenced their upbringing and location. In this pictorial reality, winged creatures can stand alongside men under palm trees. This is also evidence of cubism's continued influence on contemporary artists. The canvas has been replaced by the monitor, but it is still an arena where anything is possible and the artists can interpret their own reality.

## Summary

The works of art discussed in this chapter show the schools and movements of the twentieth century that were primarily concerned with the use and application of color.

In modern art, color could be used for color's sake without any thought to its relationship to nature or the natural world. It was a liberating time of experimentation in which the sole subject of a work of art could be its color and use of color. In some instances, even the traditional paintbrush was abandoned in favor of alternative methods of applying paint, including dripping, pouring, or staining into the fabric of the canvas. As the century progressed, some artists returned to more naturalistic applications of color. This resurgence continues to this day with computer-generated works of art. With the advent of the computer, artists were also freed from the limitations of working on canvas. The monitor and the Internet open new realms and avenues for expression, with the only limitations being the limited size of the color space.

**Figure 9-1.**
*The New York Times* now uses full-color images on a daily basis. Notice how your eye moves from the largest color image, which is directly under the masthead, to the medium size color image below it, and then back up to the smaller color image on the left. This creates a circular motion, which keeps the viewer involved and scanning the page.

Color and design are natural partners because color is a common element in good design. It is used to emphasize and accent the features of a design or product, and it can make a product better, more usable, or more pleasing to the eye. Since color has the ability to generate an unconscious response from viewers, it can influence viewers' ideas about products, graphics, or advertising. Therefore, color choices are based upon the person's sex, age, and economic status. Before viewers realize it, they are hooked by the color, and, in fact, more than half of a person's choice in purchasing a product is based solely on its color. So the color selected by a designer can make, or break, a product.

As design students, you may make color choices that are more personal rather than making choices with the general public in mind. You may want to please other designers, your classmates, or your professor. This is acceptable because a student's first portfolio of work is aimed at senior artists, art directors, and creative directors. In the real world, however, a focus group, an industrial psychologist, or even a color-forecasting service may determine the color. The personal choice of the designer may have little to do with the color of the final product. Yet designers can have an influence on the color of the final product if they know how color works and how to discuss color with clients and other design professionals.

Color grabs attention. Studies have shown that on the average, a reader will spend a fraction of a second scanning a black-and-white ad on a page. If the same ad is produced in full color, the viewer will spend at least two seconds or more viewing it. Color also captures the eye and holds it. The longer you can keep the viewer's attention, the better chance you have of getting your message across. These studies further showed that the eye is drawn to large color images. The viewer's eye will scan across the page and move in size order from the largest color image to the smallest, and then back to the text. Color also aids recall and retention. A color ad generates four times more memory retention than the same ad in black and white.

How important is color? Just ask *The New York Times*. For years the "old gray lady," as it was known, kept to its traditional format of black-and-white photos on its front page. The *Times* cautiously tested the waters by using color images in their Sunday supplement's travel and arts sections. Some worried that this would signal a change in the paper's serious nature and its reputation for in-depth coverage of the news. The reason for this concern was that previously only the tabloid-style papers such as *USA Today* used color extensively, and they were not known for their critical news coverage or journalistic integrity.

But late in 1997, the *Times* began using full-color photos on its front page (Figure 9-1). The idea, according to one editor, was to make the paper more accessible and easier to read. The use of color was part of the evolution of the paper, or as another editor explained, the idea was to redesign the paper for a new generation of readers and advertisers. This was important because studies had shown that fewer and fewer young people were reading the *Times*, and readership means money. At the same time, new digital technology made full-color printing cost-effective and easier. The underlying concept was that color could capture the attention of a whole new generation of readers who were used to color from the Internet, television, and video games. Color in newspapers has now become the norm, and even the conservative *Wall Street Journal* now uses color.

## Design and the Fine Arts

The fine arts have had a major impact on design. Many designers started out as fine art students before developing an interest in more commercially viable fields. And, in turn, advertising has influenced the fine arts. Andy Warhol's Campbell's soup cans and Brillo boxes are derived directly from package design and consumerism. This exchange of ideas has been in evidence for more than 150 years now and is not likely to stop anytime soon. Artists have even commandeered computers, which were once the sole domain of designers.

## Barbara Kruger

The relationship between design and the fine arts is evident in the work of Barbara

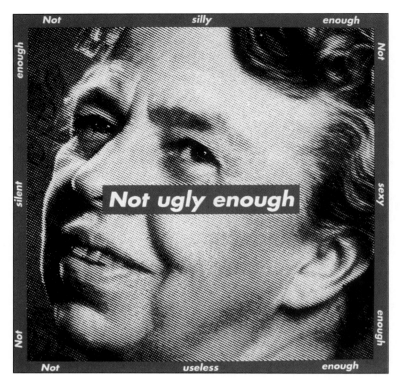

**Figure 9-2.**
Barbara Kruger,
*Untitled (Not Ugly
Enough)*, 1997.
(Courtesy of Mary
Boone Gallery,
New York.)
Framing the image in
red helps to focus our
attention and isolates the
image. The white text on
a red banner background
creates very readable
type and is a signature
element in Kruger's
work. The use of banner
boxes or headlines is
directly appropriated
from advertising and
newspaper graphics.

Kruger. She uses elements of advertising and type in her large-scale pieces and installations and addresses the issues of power, sexuality, and identity. Trained in art and design, she worked as an art director at *Mademoiselle* magazine and was later promoted to head designer. Using a "vernacular of signage" as she calls it, Kruger creates large works and installations that juxtapose words or slogans and images, creating a visual dichotomy. The strong feminist underpinning of her work is evident in *Untitled (Not Ugly Enough)*, Figure 9-2. Kruger uses her trademark white text on a red banner. This use of text directly relates to mass communication as seen in billboards and advertising.

### The Sixties: Psychedelic Color

There was a resurgence of the primacy of color in the late 1960s and early 1970s. The psychedelic colors used for posters and clothing made a bold statement for the times. Color was used not only to grab attention, but also to say "we are different from you."

The "you" in this case was the establishment including parents, teachers, and authority figures from police to politicians. The counter-culture of young people used color in everything from tie-dyed clothing to posters to make a statement and to stand out. The statement was "I am different. I'm an individual." Color was an effective part of this philosophy because at that time men tended to dress alike in dull blue or gray business suits with the overriding credo to fit in and go along with the group.

Wes Wilson captured the spirit of the counterculture in his work. He created posters for the Filmore West and Avalon Ballroom, run by music legend impresario Bill Graham. His creations were more than just announcements of who was playing on a given evening, but bold visual color statements. Wilson used vibrating complements to create shimmering effects of movement in his work. People avidly collected and displayed his work in their homes. He could be viewed as a modern-era Toulouse-Lautrec with the major difference being that the majority of Wilson's work was created solely with color and type. In Figure 9-3, the complementary hues of red and green work together with the imagery of the fire and make up the letters of the names of the bands that would be playing that evening. The vibration of the hues (which is caused by the complementary hues that are very close in value and saturation) creates the upward movement and works in concert with the direction of the type that is created to look like flames.

### April Greiman

As one of the founders of the postmodern movement, along with others such as David Carson, April Greiman changed the face of design. Type no longer had to be sharp and legible, but could be used solely as design elements. It could be

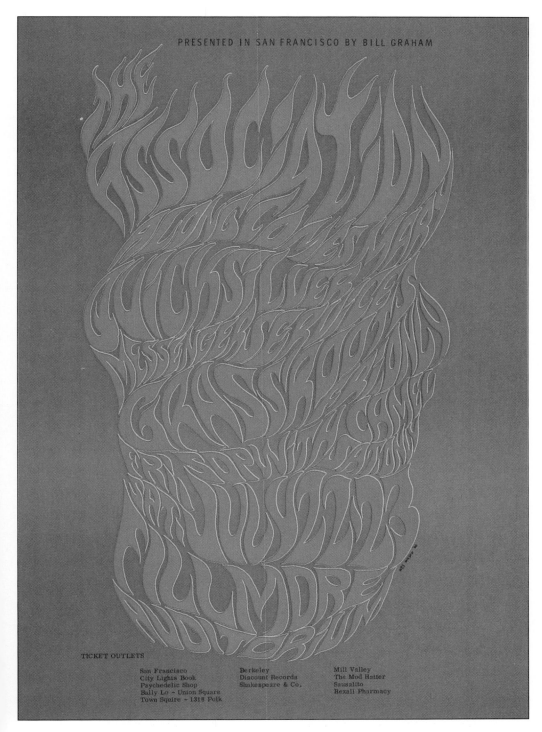

**Figure 9-3.**
Wes Wilson,
*Poster,* 1966.
Bill Graham
Archives, LLC.
Wilson often designed
his own type and used
complementary color
schemes for their visual
vibration. This meant the
hues he selected had to
be close in value and
saturation to create the
vibrating visual effects.

roughed up, rotated, and faded out, the same holds true for her use of color. Greiman was one of the leading proponents of the Macintosh computer. She believes that the computer is not merely an instrument but an intelligent tool, which means that it can be a viable part of the design process. And hers is a process-oriented approach. In her poster *Does it Make Sense?* from the No. 133

**Figure 9-4.**
April Greiman, *Does it Make Sense?* No. 133 issue of *Design Quarterly.* This piece is interesting because it can be viewed from any orientation. There really is no top or bottom. The use of the monochromatic color scheme unifies the divergent visual elements.

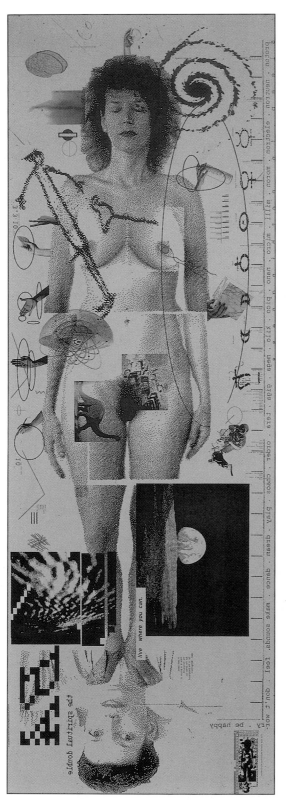

issue of *Design Quarterly* (Figure 9-4), Greiman created a personal statement with a nude self-portrait. What could be more personal than that? She uses a monochromatic range of blue as a unifying element to the vast array of shapes, textures, and images used in the piece. When Greiman travels, she carries a plastic box to collect a variety of materials to add to her palette of colors and textures. These collected souvenirs then find their way into her work.

## Graphics and Brand Identity

As we have seen previously, many of our reactions to color are learned responses. Red for "stop" and green for "go" are things we are taught by our parents to keep us safe and to protect us. Society reinforces these regulations to create rules for an orderly society and to keep people safe. But these are not the only ways that we learn to associate color with an idea or practice. Branding, or brand identity, is also a learned response. Commercials in both print and television condition us to recognize a symbol (a logo) and its color with the name of the company. With the addition of the Internet and pop-up windows that advertise every imaginable product, we are constantly bombarded with images of products and their names and logos. Each company has its own color or color scheme that is burned into our brains. If you don't believe it's true, ask any four-year-old to name several companies, and he or she will be able to tell you the color and shape of logo for each one. When companies are successful, they no longer need to have their names in their logo—the shape and color are all that are required. How many companies can you name by just seeing their logo?

To preserve this color identity, many companies use the PANTONE MATCHING SYSTEM® (Figure 9-5). Also known as spot colors, these are specially mixed inks that will produce an exact hue, including the specific saturation and value. These inks may cost more, but they ensure the color consistency, which is at the heart of brand identity. If the color of a product varies even slightly, it will break the unconscious psychological connection with the customer or viewer. This brief split second is enough time for the people to reconsider their purchase. For most of our purchases we are on "automatic pilot," grabbing up the product without ever giving it a second thought.

## Package Design

The package for a product may be as important as, if not more important than, the product itself. If the package is not alluring and inviting, the product will never be purchased. The color of a product (and its packaging) becomes synonymous with the product itself. PANTONE colors are used in product packaging to ensure that the color identity is maintained across geographic regions.

Color recognition is important because people reach for a product based on its color before they consciously read the name of the item on the package. If the color was not exactly the same, the visual difference would stop the purchaser for even a fraction of a second. In that time, the buyer would have enough time to think about their selection, possibly changing their mind and selecting another product instead.

What do you think are the most popular colors for packaging in the United States? Red, white, and blue. The underlying theme of patriotism helps to sell the product. The subtle message in the use of these colors is that the product is all-American. Take a walk down the aisle at the grocery store and really look at the colors of the packages. Complementary pairs, especially red and green, are the next choice. Contrary to

popular belief, red and green are not just Christmas colors. They are used to sell everything from salad dressing to hair spray. Legibility and contrast are key factors in labeling. While yellow and black are the most visible, they are rarely used because of their connotations to danger, stinging bees, and so on. As illustrated in Figure 9-6, black on white followed by red, green, or blue on white are also easy to read and easy on the eyes. The least legible and hardest color combinations to read include red on blue, white on red, black on green, and orange on blue. Strong contrast in large type may be acceptable and stand out smartly, but it is not used on small type, or what is commonly known as body copy. In addition, hues close in value or saturation are also hard to read. This is one reason why analogous groups are rarely used in type and packaging.

Economic conditions also play a major role in product design and color selection. Color clearly reflects the financial condition of an era. Flashy bold colors are signs of great economic prosperity. The 1920s and 1980s are both prime examples, where color is

**Figure 9-5.**
The PANTONE® formula guide. (Image provided courtesy of Pantone, Inc. PANTONE® and the PANTONE MATCHING SYSTEM® are the property of Pantone, Inc.) There are actually several types of color formulas, including coated, uncoated, metallic, and pastel inks. They are the most commonly used brand of spot color inks and are employed in graphics, packaging, and products.

Some color combinations are easy to read.
Some color combinations are easy to read.

Some color combinations are easy to read.

Some color combinations are harder to read

Some color combinations are harder to read

Some color combinations are harder to read

And some are almost impossible.

And some are almost impossible.

And some are almost impossible.

**Figure 9-6.**
An illustration of the readability of color and type. The greater the contrast, the easier it is to read. As the background color and the color of the type become closer in hue or value, they are more difficult to read. Analogous color schemes do not work well for this reason.

**Figure 9-7.**
Poison Tendre perfume by Christian Dior, 2003. The new red color gives the perfume a contemporary look. The underlying associations of the apple and Eve are used to convey the idea that this perfume could be a bit dangerous. The underlying message would not be as effective with another color. Red adds to the sensuality and passion that Dior wants to convey.

viewed as disposable and used as fashion statements. In a booming economy, high-key colors are used to show the opulence of the owner. In times of economic uncertainty or recession, a more subdued palette is used. Classic colors that people will want to live with for long periods of time have also become popular. The products created have

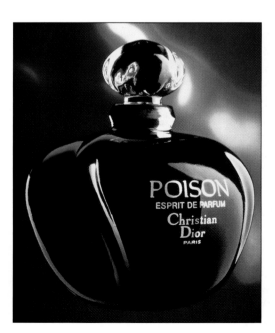

clean lines, and the use of white, blue, and black increase substantially.

## A Fragrance is Born

It is rare that a company begins the design process of a product by starting with the selection of its color, but such was the case with a new perfume by Christian Dior. A deep emerald green was the starting point for Poison. The new fragrance was developed and geared to a young audience. In fragrances, the color green (usually a very light version of the hue) was normally associated with citrus and lime scents. Christian Dior selected the deep vibrant green hue to go with the shocking new name, as well as to set it apart from all the perfumes on the market. The deep green color was selected to remind the user of emeralds. The bottle and packaging design came next. The two-tone tortoiseshell design on the package created an exclusive look. The fragrance was then developed with a combination of oriental and floral scents. It possesses a blend of amber, honey, berries, and other spices and because of its strong nature, is recommended for evening use.

In 2003, Dior announced a change to Poison perfume. The traditional deep green was being replaced with a bright intense red. The change was to bring the perfume up to date for a new market. In a recent press release, they use the following: bewitching red, forbidden fruit, enticing serpent. The allusions to the Garden of Eden are quite clear. The new color of the perfume is the color of the apple. The underlying message is that the color and its fragrance are irresistible, and if you use it, you will be as well.

## Product Design

Apple revolutionized the computer with its iMac (Figure 9-8). It was the first computer to be sold in colors, since up to this point all computers sold were an institutional gray or

**Figure 9-8.**
Jonathan Ive,
the iMac, 1998.
Ive's design team made
a bold move in creating
the first computer in
five different colors.
The colors are bright,
saturated hues, which
contrast nicely with the
pure white of the base.

putty color. They were a purely utilitarian machine, and aesthetics were never an issue. Apple changed the face of selling computers with its low-cost iMac, and the visionary behind this move was Jonathan Ive and his design team. He felt that this was the meeting of technology and the individual. The idea was to change the very meaning of the object. By changing its color, Apple moved the personal computer from the industrial to personal. Their concept was to make the computer relevant to daily life. The computer could now be seen as

furniture not to be hidden away, but as part of the room décor. By offering the computer in five colors, it could be marketed to both sexes and all age groups.

As other companies such as Dell jumped on board, Apple continued to experiment with different color combinations. They extended this concept of color to their laptop computer models, and the iBook was born. The higher-end versions of these machines were offered in Graphite, a dark gray. This color appealed to a more business-conscious

**Figure 9-9.**
Jonathan Ive, the New
iMac, 2003.
The shape of the base is
echoed in the form of the
twin stereo speakers. All
of the corners, from the
monitor to the keyboard,
have been rounded off as
well. The use of an
absolute pure white
again separated Apple
from the rest of the pack.

**Figure 9-10.**
Lunar Design,
*Oral-B CrossAction
Toothbrush*, 1999.
The new color scheme
updates the product and
is slightly reminiscent of
the iMac. Even the
bristles of the brush
are colored to work
with the color of the
handle to create a unified
contemporary design.

client who might be embarrassed to be seen owning a bright orange or green computer. As more companies brought their own versions of colored computers to the market, Ive and his design team changed gears and redesigned the iMac with a flat screen and hemisphere base in a matte sanded white finish called snow (Figure 9-9).

Not only were computers redesigned, but also mundane items such as the toothbrush were overhauled and revamped. The toothbrush, an item that most people consider to be purely utilitarian, was redesigned to enhance both its function and its look. The Lunar Design group of Palo Alto, California, was hired by Oral-B to undertake this venture. The bristles were relocated to crisscross each other and to enhance its scrubbing and cleaning capabilities. The product's new brand name was *CrossAction* (Figure 9-10). Their concept was to connect the design technology with the brand name, so that the style of the new instrument would become synonymous with the company's name. The team designed an ergonomic handle with serrated finger grips and an elongated oval handgrip. The two-toned color scheme used was vaguely reminiscent of the duo-tone design of the iMac computer.

The colored sections of the brush handle were made of translucent colored plastic and make a nice counterpoint to the white opaque stem. This style began cropping up in everything from tabletop cooking grills to microwave ovens. Even the Mini Cooper has a similar two-tone styling.

**Toy Design**

Toy designing is not a game, but a serious business. The color used for a particular game or plaything is based both on the function of the toy and the recommended age range. Bright, simple primary hues are used for toddlers. As a rule, toys for girls still employ a soft, warm range of colors and pastel hues. On the other hand, toys for boys are usually made with brighter, more saturated hues, especially blues and bright reds. Sexual stereotyping begins at an early age. Wilder hues and color combinations are used for teens that are trying to assert their independence. Color is another means for teens to assert their control on their environment and self-image. One of the underlying elements is choosing colors that their parents will not particularly like, to reinforce the notion of independence and autonomy. Color combinations become more complex as the age range for the product increases.

Jesse DeStasio, a toy designer and animator, was faced with a design dilemma when his character Rex Ganon was going to make its debut in the established line of Plan B Special Forces figures. His color scheme for the figure was important to ensure that it would fit in with the rest of the existing line. Rex's clothing was reminiscent of World War 2 uniforms, so he decided to work with a more subdued color palette. DeStasio decided on the red jacket, which he says added a nice spark to the figure, as well as fitting in with the time period. He used PANTONE shades for his colors, as seen in

Figure 9-11, because of the language barriers in dealing with overseas production. As he said, "It's tough for a Chinese worker to understand 'Mulberry,' but PANTONE 492c is universal." The four PANTONE color swatches are noted on the final drawing. By doing so, there can be no confusion regarding the designer's choice of color. Using these spot colors ensures that wherever the figure is produced, the color will remain consistent and true. The photographs of the final figure produced can be seen in the press release for the toy line, in Figure 9-12.

## Web Sites

The newest method of distributing information and advertising to a mass audience is the Internet. Formally know as Bitnet, the Net was once a computer network for people in education and the military. Its explosion of popularity began in the 1990s and was spurred on by the accessibility and

**Figure 9-11.**
Jesse DeStasio, Rex Ganon action figure, 2003. The work starts out as a sketch on a page. It is scanned in, and in this case, he uses Photoshop to add the color, which allows him to pick and choose from several shades in order to get the right one. PANTONE colors are used to ensure accuracy and consistency in reproduction.

**Figure 9-12.**
Jesse DeStasio, Rex Ganon action figure, 2003. The press release for the action figure shows the last step in the design process. The figure can now be marketed and shipped to toy stores.

**Figure 9-13.**
The Adobe color picker with the Web-safe color option selected. It makes selecting colors for the Web as easy as pointing and clicking. (Courtesy of Adobe Systems, Inc.)

affordability of personal computers to the general public. The Internet is now a worldwide phenomenon, with Internet cafés in every distant part of the globe. Cyberspace is a universal domain not bound by any culture or country. Since colors have both regional and cultural associations, you must plan out and research your color choice before finalizing the site.

While the Internet has become one of the largest communications mechanisms—literally spanning the world—the color space it uses is quite small. Of the millions of colors the human eye can see or a computer can display, there are only 256 colors available to artists and designers for the Web. Creating Web-safe color is no longer the chore it once was. Most software programs, such as Adobe's Photoshop and Illustrator, have built-in Web color pickers (Figure 9-13).

Each of the Web's 256 colors has a related numeric value, which not only stands for the actual hue, but also its size and the amount of memory it uses. Black uses the least digital space and has a numeric value of 0. All other colors are larger and take up more space and computer memory. This is an important factor to remember because Web designers must work with files or image sizes that are relatively small. The larger the file size, the longer it will take a Web page to open. By

limiting the palette to 256 colors, speed is achieved. Size limitations and opening speed take the place of color complexity on the Web. Users won't wait for your page to open, and not everyone has a high-speed digital subscriber line (DSL). Even though most users are still using slower modem hookups, there are a few ways around the issues of speed. Several small images can be used or one large image can be cut up into several pieces and **tiled** together to allow for faster page opening.

## Color Complexity

Studies have shown that when the image and site complexity were not sufficient, users lost interest and moved on. But complexity doesn't mean confusion—viewers were also turned off by visual information that was not presented clearly. Confusing sites can interfere with cognitive processing, which means understanding the aim of the site. The use of animation also had positive effects on attention, perceived interest, and users' attitudes toward the brand portrayed. Color complexity also had positive effects on viewers' attention span as well as their intention to purchase the items shown.

## Animation and Motion Graphics

The animator is in an interesting position—sometimes considered a designer and at other times an artist. The skill set employed is the same, only the person's intention creates the difference.

One of the most important color relationships for animators is the use of warm and cool colors. Since the computer's range of color or color space is much larger than that of film or videotape, animators are sometimes forced to work within a narrower scope of hues. By understanding the push and pull of color temperature, animators can select hues that will work off each other. One basic method is to place cool hues in the

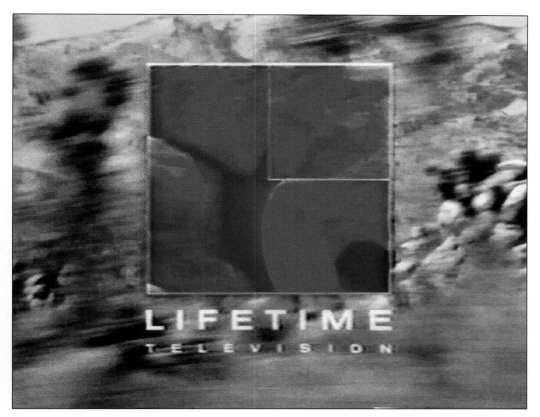

**Figure 9-14.**
April Greiman, Lifetime TV Identity Spot, 1987. The cooler blue and green of the background appear to visually move to the back and push the warm red box to the foreground. The well-planned use of color can enhance the visual dynamics.

**Figure 9-15.**
*The Game Room*, Exodus Entertainment. Here reverse contrast is used. The background includes lighter, softer tints, while the main character in the foreground is composed of deep blues and violets. The use of this color scheme helps to isolate the figure from the background, as well as focusing our attention on the main character.

background and the warmer ones on the foreground or main character. Since cool colors appear to recede in space, they push the background farther back and create a deeper sense of space. The warm colors used for the foreground elements allow them to stand out more from the background and visually appear to push forward on the picture plane or screen. This same concept also applies to other film and video elements, such as motion graphics. April Greiman used this color combination of a cool blue background and the warm reds in her TV spot for the Lifetime Network (Figure 9-14).

Contrast is also a concern for the animator. If the colors selected are too close in hue, value, or saturation, the images will not stand out on screen. For example, analogous color schemes tend to blend into one another and become harder to be seen. Another form of contrast regularly used is desaturated colors for the background and more highly saturated hues for the foreground. This concept is clearly illustrated in Figure 9-15, a scene from *The Game Room*.

## Summary

The choice of color can make or break a design. Studies have shown that it may be the single most important factor when a consumer selects an item for purchase. It acts as a magnet by drawing the eye and can be used to create a focal point. Color trends change with the times and are constantly evolving. The artist and designer must understand that culture and technology affect attitudes regarding color. As technological advances occur, new colors and new forms of color are made available to the designer. The Internet and the mass acceptance of digital technology have opened up new avenues for color expression.

Designers must constantly update their palette to keep pace with market expectations, and all products must be designed with color in mind. The public has become savvy and more sophisticated when it comes to color, and designers must keep pushing the envelope to make their work stand out and be noticed.

**The Future of Color: Chapter 10**

**Figure 10-1.**
Winsor & Newton
water-mixable oil colors.
Turpentine is no longer
required—they clean up
with just soap and water.
(Courtesy of Winsor
& Newton.)

The future of color is now.

Color is a part of our ever-changing world. The ways we create and use color are constantly evolving. New technologies bring advances in our application and use of color, and the Internet and progress in such divergent areas as virtual realities and cybernetics are changing our ideas regarding the very nature of what color is and can be. But it is not just through high-tech research that innovation occurs. There are low-tech and no-tech advances in theory, practice, and convention. Even our courts and the rule of law play a role in how we work with and use color.

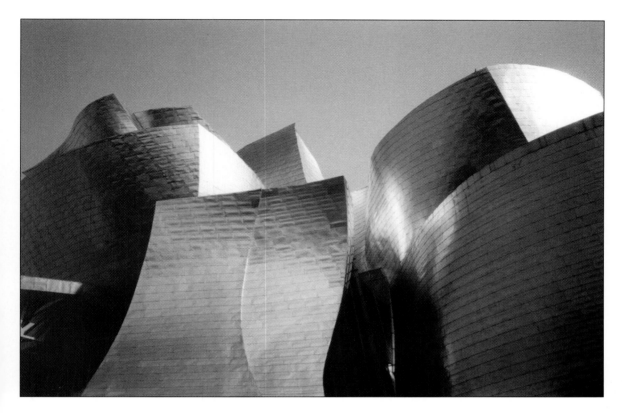

## Environmentally Friendly Paints

Not all advances in color involve digital technology. Even in traditional media, new advances are being made. The push for nontoxic, environmentally friendly materials will continue. Artists want to try to minimize the health-related illnesses caused by the materials they work with and that have historically plagued the art and design fields. Nontoxic inks for etching and printing have grown in popularity. In the last few years, Winsor & Newton has introduced water-mixable oil colors to the market. Their advantage to traditional oil paints is that they do not require turpentine to clean brushes and other materials—they clean up with plain soap and water. This eliminates the fire hazard of oil- and turpentine-soaked rags, as well as the noxious smell. According to the manufacturer, hog hair brushes are advised for a heavy impasto of paint, while thinner coats normally used for glazing require a soft-haired brush.

## Color and Architecture

New materials such as titanium are being used to revolutionize architecture. The single most recognizable building of the new millennium is the Guggenheim Museum in Bilbao, Spain (Figure 10-2). Designed by architect Frank Gehry, it has an organic feel of something that has sprouted rather than been constructed. The building has completely changed the region by making it a new tourist destination, and it is credited with the economic rebirth of the Basque region. Surveys have shown that 80 percent of the visitors to the area are there to see the museum. This type of signature architecture has come to represent the city in the same way the Opera House has come to symbolize Sydney, Australia. These buildings are immediately recognizable and have become icons of their respective cities.

While the museum started as a sketch on paper, it was transferred to a digital medium and engineered with the help of three-

**Figure 10-2.**
Frank Gehry, *Guggenheim Museum*, Bilbao, Spain. Copyright FMGB Bilbao, Spain. Photograph by Steven Bleicher. All rights reserved. Total or partial reproduction is prohibited.
A view of the museum as seen at midday. The bright sunlight creates a golden cast to the metal skin of the building. The blue of the surrounding water is also reflected in the shimmering surface.

**Figure 10-3.**
Frank Gehry,
*Guggenheim Museum*,
Bilbao, Spain.
Copyright FMGB
Bilbao, Spain.
Photograph by Steven
Bleicher. All rights
reserved. Total or
partial reproduction
is prohibited.
In the late afternoon sun,
the colors of the building
change to a variety of
deep oranges and reds.
Violet is also reflected
from the surrounding
water. The building
seems to change color
like a chameleon.

dimensional computer-modeling programs.
The metal used to fabricate the outside—
titanium—works like a skin. Because of the
complexity of the curved surfaces, the CAD
programs ensured that each part would fit
together and that the half-millimeter thick
metal membrane would fit onto each block.
Gehry says that the bottom section of the
building is kind of a boat shape, while the
titanium panels remind visitors of the scales
of a fish. The water that surrounds part of
the structure further reinforces these aquatic
allusions. The metal surface reflects light and
seems to change color depending upon the
time of day and weather conditions. In Figures
10-2 and 10-3, the color of the water and sky
resonate in the polished metal skin of the
building. The ever-changing façade is as much
a draw as the artwork inside the museum.

### Color Ownership: Color and the Law

In a sense, there are really only a limited
number of colors or hues, or at least ones that

can be reproduced in printing, packaging,
and products. As advertising and product
branding increasingly encroach on daily life,
people are bombarded with advertisements
and product placement in everything from
movies to elevators, as well as all of the pop-
ups on the Internet. The colors and names
of products are so closely associated that
consumers often reach for a product by the
visual color cues of its packaging. With each
company seeking to claim colors for themselves and their products, legal disputes are
bound to arise. The question of whether
a color can be so closely associated with a
specific product that no other manufacturer
can use it is litigated regularly.

Colors are used to identify products, and
certain hues can become synonymous with
a particular brand of merchandise. If companies were allowed to wholly copyright colors
and their usage, the remaining few left for new
products would be sorely limited. Notice the
minute differences between the colors used on

labels and packages. These slight variations are enough for your eye to distinguish the color differences and therefore for the manufacturers to be happy that you will not reach for the wrong product. So why do some products use the same basic coloring for their labels? Take, for example, Banquet frozen fried chicken and Ore-Ida frozen toaster hash browns. The basic body of the box on each is the same shade of bright red. The main differences are that the boxes are in vastly different sizes and each has a large image of the product on the front of the package. There is very little chance you will pick up the wrong item by mistake. Additionally, since they are completely different food products, they are not in competition with each other.

Most of us remember LifeSavers candies from our childhood. That distinctive multi-colored package with the red, yellow, orange and green bands of color hinted to the fruit flavors inside (Figure 10-4). The Curtiss Candy Company came out with a similar, multicolored stripe package for a round disk-shaped, fruit-flavored candy. LifeSavers sued Curtiss, saying they had the sole market use of the multicolored striped package and that the colored bands were synonymous with their candy. The courts ruled against LifeSavers, saying that there was no trade-mark infringement. The ruling stated that the use of this type of multicolored packaging was the "general practice of the trade" and the coloring was descriptive of the flavors of the candy. Since the coloring of the package directly related to the flavors of the candy inside, it could not be trademarked.

In another case, Dap, which makes building and construction supplies, sold ceramic tile adhesive (as well as many of its other adhesives) packages with red labels (Figure 10-5). When rival Color Tile Manufacturing, Inc. came out with a similarly colored packaging for their version of the same type of product, Dap "saw

red." They filed suit, and the courts ruled in their favor. So how was this different from the LifeSavers case? The decision said that red was not intrinsically related to that product nor was it descriptive of its function or use. Flavor was not an issue here. Therefore, when Color Tile used a similar red for their product packaging, they were infringing on the "secondary meaning" of the color red that was associated with Dap in the minds of consumers. The use of

**Figure 10-4.**
LifeSavers candies, a roll of fruit-flavored candies. The multicolored stripes on the LifeSavers package shows the consumer the flavors of the candies in the roll. The company uses different-colored packaging depending upon the flavor of the candy.

**Figure 10-5.**
Dap adhesive. The color of the red package has nothing to do with the product inside. It was selected for visibility and product identification and not product function.

the color red was not related to the color of the product, its use, or its flavor, as in the LifeSavers case, so there was no valid reason for the another company to choose red for their package.

A specific color may receive protection, but the courts realize there should be limits. When a color is so closely associated to a specific brand of a product, it may be protected. However, colors such as green are associated with a vast number of products, from citrus to mint flavors and even peanut butter. Therefore, a company trying to trademark a specific green hue would have a much harder time stating their case for trademark protection. The courts have also said that if the use of a specific color was related to the "functionality" of a product, it could not be trademarked, as in the case of fertilizers that use blue packaging to show they contain nitrate. But even in these cases, the manufacturer of the color in question must be able to show that it has used that particular hue for a long enough and extended period of time for the general public to wholly associate that color to the specific brand of the product. The trademark laws are just vague enough when it comes to the issue of color to keep lawyers busy for years to come.

Will you be able to use that particular hue in your painting, animation, or game? Or will you have to check with a legal clearinghouse before you apply the paint to the canvas or select a hue with your computer's color picker?

It's doubtful it will ever come to this and that things will go so far afield. It is certain, however, that color will no longer be the sole purview of the artist and designer. We are going to have to share our palette with a wide variety of folks because color is one of the most defining elements of our life and universe.

## The Web

New file formats will afford better and more accurate color for the Web. Currently, most file formats used on the Internet (GIF and JPEG) do not have the capacity to carry information on gamma and chromaticity. New file formats such as JPEG 2000, though still under development, will be able to carry this essential color information. But currently most Web browsers cannot read this information. This ability is being developed for new browsers and as of this date only Microsoft Explorer for the Macintosh has the capacity to read these types of profiles that are built into Web graphics. However, a new graphics format known as PNG, or portable network graphics, can store this type of information for improved color reproduction and matching. It is designed to work on all platforms and most Web browsers. The ICC, the International Color Consortium, is also hard at work on developing new graphic file formats with enhanced data storage capacity. So, the future goal for the Web is more precise and dramatically improved color reproduction.

## New Territory

Digital technology will remain an ever-increasing influence in the coming years. At its inception in the early 1980s, many people sought to write off this new technology as a fad and said it would never catch on, let alone last. Now the only question is: what's next? New fields have been created—from computer animation to games to virtual realities—that are so sophisticated that the images on screen could pass for the real thing.

Artists and their ever-inquisitive search for new forms to make art have grabbed onto the computer and other new media such as lasers and holography. For some, technology is used as a tool to create their work, while to others the technology itself has become their principle medium.

This combination of high technology and art has not really produced a new movement or "-ism." However, it has opened up the boundaries of what it is possible to make art with. It is not one single medium, but a host of mediums mixed together to form a new means of creating art. Artists are now able to make art and interact with the viewer on a new grand scale. In the past, the audience has played a passive role in viewing art. Now with the use of motion-capture devices and sensors, the audience becomes an important element of the artwork itself.

In these new ways of visualizing space, the computer becomes the pigment for this type of artist in the same way da Vinci used oils. The artists creating these works do not consider themselves techno-artists, but simply artists who are working in a new medium and who mix mediums. These artists have not completely abandoned traditional concerns. They are still involved in figure/ground relationships as their traditional media counterparts, but now the ground is the screen or actual space.

## High-Definition Television

One of the most dramatic changes to the field of color that will affect our daily life will be the move from the current standard format television to high-definition television (HDTV) (Figure 10-6). This move, which is currently being phased in over the next few years, will affect every household. Both broadcast and cable stations are gearing up for the switch. It is becoming more common to see the informational promotion at the start of a program announcing to viewers that the show they are about to watch is being broadcast in high definition. The higher resolution of these new television sets and the related broadcast capabilities will allow for a greater and more dynamic range of hues to be displayed. HDTV has the same full-color attributes as film. Issues such as banding and bleeding will be eliminated. Artists and designers will be able to use a full, open palette without restrictions and create richer production values, further adding to the overall entertainment experience.

## Lasers and Holography

The term *laser* stands for light amplifications by stimulated emission

**Figure 10-6.**
Panasonic high-definition television (HDTV).
Image courtesy of Panasonic. Notice how the television screen is wider than a traditional analog television screen and is more reminiscent of a movie theater. The HD broadcast also has a larger color space, which affords the viewer a more intense picture with even more lifelike color.

**Figure 10-7.**
Katalin Sallai,
*His Story*, 1994.
Sallai feels she can only
obtain the deep acid
green she wanted for
the figures inside the
cross by using holo-
graphy and chose it first
and foremost because of
the intensity of the color.

radiation. The basic principle of a laser is that light can be intensified and made to amplify itself to such a degree that it could burn a hole in a diamond. The first lasers were created in 1960, and the technology has been advancing steadily ever since. To create a laser, a beam of light is shot through a hollow gas-filled tube. The ends are reflective and the beam of light bounces back and forth between the ends of the reflective chambers until they develop into a wavelength of tremendous intensity.

The color of the laser beam is related to the gas used. Red is the most commonly used and is created using helium-neon gas. Krypton gas can produce the widest range of colors, including red, green, yellow, and blue. Since laser beams can travel great distances without spreading out, they are used in outdoor shows and have even been experimented with to replace fireworks. Once lasers were expensive, but today they are used in pointers and many other devices.

Another use for lasers is in holography. The term comes from the Greek word *holos* and means whole or complete, and *gram* meaning message. The image itself is referred to as a hologram, while the complete process is called holography. It is the process of holding and displaying a three-dimensional image on a photographic plate or light-sensitive media. Holography is composed of two parts: creating the hologram and illuminating it to show the image. To do this, a beam of laser light is reflected off the subject onto a light-sensitive media. Then another laser beam, known as the reference beam, is shined onto the plate. Where the beams cross, they create a complex pattern of stripes and illuminate the image. The hologram changes the direction of the light waves in the beam so that they seem to come from the original subject. This creates a three-dimensional image that appears to float in space.

Katalin Sallai is one of a number of artists that use lasers in the form of holography in their artwork. She feels that the color the laser produces in the hologram is very unique and that she cannot achieve it in any other media. In *His Story* (Figure 10-7), Sallai feels that the bright green color of the hologram represents terror, while the lighter greens and blues of the outer image represent a poisonous atmosphere that works in a homogenous manner with the deep intense green of the cross. The cross itself is made up of several images of Christ and Mary. Mary is slightly out of focus to symbolize what Sallai believes—women are treated as second-class citizens in society.

## Web Art

John Weber calls the Internet the "wild card" in the world of art. Egalitarian by its very nature, there is no admission charge or need to fly to a distant land to see an individual artwork. The art is wherever you are—online and hooked up to the Internet. Mark Napier is one of a number of new artists who are producing artwork specifically for the Web. Napier's Web site, *Potatoland,* at http://www.potatoland.org/,

**Figure 10-8.**
Mark Napier,
*Grass (a subsection
of USA)*, 2003.
Medium: Java, Perl,
Images of Grass.
URL:
http://potatoland.org/
words/grass.
Since his images are
reproduced for viewers
on their home monitors,
a more intimate space is
created. The greens he
used remind the viewer
of the range of color
that can be seen in a
meadow of grass from
new yellow-green to the
dying brown hues.

is a vast collection of all his online artwork.
It includes projects from *USA* to the *Digital
Landfill,* to name a few.

*Grass,* which is a part or subsection of
*USA,* starts out with a somewhat blank
screen, and then begins to fill with green
lines of color placed on an angle. The screen
continues to fill with these green lines and
as the screen fills, the shade of green
changes. This color shift spans the full range
of the hue working in an analogous scheme.
The color also shifts into various green
neutrals. These color shifts (figure 10–8)
remind the viewer of the change of seasons.
In one shift, they move from a very light
yellow-green through a midgreen, reminding
the viewers of spring. In another, the grass
forms begin to turn brown, signaling the
coming of fall.

## Virtual Reality and Interactivity

Virtual realities have been around for
a number of years, but they are still in their
infancy. In the past they have been used

as simulators and trainers for pilots, the
military, police, and doctors. Newer uses
include theme rides at the nation's top
amusement parks. But they have also long
been the area of exploration for artists.
They are a place to experiment with visuals,
sound, and interactivity. In this type of art,
the audience is no longer merely viewing,
but is actively participating in the artwork.
Without the audience interaction, there is
no art. The art is in the interaction.

Char Davies has completed two major
interactive artworks. Her most recent,
*Ephémère,* is a fully interactive visual and
aural virtual artwork. The work uses real-
time 3-D computer graphics and interactive
3-D sound. The immersant (no longer merely
a viewer as in traditional forms of art) dons
a stereoscopic head mounted display and
real-time motion tracking, which is based
on balance and breath. During the immersive
experience, visual and aural elements
develop, linger, and then transition out in
response to several variables, including pace

**Figure 10-9.**
Char Davies, *Ephémère*, 1998.
Immersive virtual environment with real-time sound and graphics.
Additional credits: Custom VR software, John Harrison. Computer graphics, Georges Mauro. Sonic architecture and programming, Dorota Blaszczak. The artist becomes a creator and manager in a work of this magnitude, which takes several individuals with diverse specialties to be able to present it. This type of art experience literally envelops the viewer (now a participant) in a unique visceral encounter. After several minutes within the work, the color and sound fade in one of several endings in which naturalist hues—neutrals of either autumn leaves, embers, or ashes—float in an empty space.

of movement, length and duration of gaze, passage of time, and more.

The piece works on three levels: the landscape, earth, and interior body. It suggests the symbolic relations between body and earth. As a Canadian, the work was inspired by an actual place on the mountain slopes of rural Quebec. This inspiration was evident in the color used in the work. Her use of strong neutrals in an analogous range of warm colors can clearly be seen in Figure 10-9. These hues bring viewers back to the natural world and are evocative of nature.

**Summary**

None of us can quite know the future of color. It will change and evolve as technology and science continue to move forward. But it is certain to say that advances will continue. Whether it is finding new uses for materials as Gehry did in the Guggenheim at Bilbao, or exploring the realms of new technology, color never stands still. But it is not only technology that will shape the future of color. Low-tech inventions have helped refine the existing art media and have made them safer to work with and use. This may open up art to new experiments from hobbyists to professionals. Legal issues will also continue to shape graphic design and advertising. Since there is only a finite number of hues, the rush to claim their providence will continue and may become more contentious.

As we have seen throughout the text, color may be one of the single most important design elements. Its future is now in your hands. Where will you take it? How will you use it? What new forms will you be able to create?

# Glossary

## A

**absolute threshold**—the minimum amount of light needed to cause a discernible visual sensation.

**achromatics**—also known as neutrals, they have no chroma or color and include black, white, and gray. Since they are not hues, they cannot be found on the color wheel.

**additive color**—mixtures of light. The additive primaries are red, green, and blue.

**afterimage**—a fleeting false image that is seen after prolonged exposure to a specific hue. The afterimage will be the complement of that hue.

**aliasing**—the jagged edge or stair-step effect seen in a digital image. What you are seeing are the actual pixels that make up the image.

**analogous colors**—three hues that are next to each other on the color wheel. On very large color wheels (forty-eight steps or more), four hues that are next to each other may be used.

**atmospheric perspective**—a visual effect caused by the diminishing light. As elements recede into deep space, they dissolve into a middle gray.

## C

**candelas**—unit of measure for the brightness of lamps.

**chrome**—a suffix meaning color or colored, as in *polychrome*.

**chromophobia**—fear of color and the use of color.

**color management profiles**—a computer-generated and assigned value or record of the color mode used in creating the image.

**color modes**—models that enable us to express color in terms of numerical values. CMYK, HSB, LAB, and RGB are examples of color modes.

**colorimeter**—a device that measures hue, luminance, and saturation.

**complementary contrast**—the effect created when two complementary hues of equal value and saturation are placed next to each other in a design.

**complements**—complementary colors that are directly opposite each other on the color wheel.

## D

**dermo-optic vision**—alternative color perception where the skin literally sees or senses the color.

**double split complementary**—two hues that are next to each other on the color wheel and their complements or opposite hues.

## F

**fovea**—the photoreceptor area in the retina that contains only cones.

**fugitive colors**—colors (paints and pigments) that fade over time due to exposure to sunlight.

## G

**gamma**—the measurement and mathematical formula of the relationship of voltage input to the relative brightness of the image seen on the screen.

**gamut**—the range of color that devices such as monitors, scanners, and printers can display or reproduce.

**guerrilla artworks**—unsponsored artworks put up without permission.

**H**

**heightened color**—the use of color without regard to the natural or local color of the object, usually used by the artist for dramatic or emotional effect.

**hue**—the actual name of a color.

**I**

**image-based lighting**—a computer algorithm that emulates how light reflects off an object and scatters over surfaces, used in animation.

**incident beam**—the beam of light coming from the light source and striking the object.

**inherent value**—the actual value of a given object.

**intermediate color**—a synonymous term for *tertiary color*, which is made by combining a primary and a secondary color.

**iodopsin**—the light-sensitive chemical agent in the cone that is believed to be involved with our ability to see color.

**L**

**local color**—the actual color of an object.

**luminaire**—the proper name for a light fixture, or what we normally call lamps.

**M**

**metamerism**—the visual phenomenon that occurs when two objects or hues appear to be the same when viewed under one light source, but appear visually different when viewed under a different light source.

**monochromatic**—a single color that includes the full range of tints, tones, and shades of that color.

**monochromatics**—people who are color blind (those who have an extremely rare vision abnormality that prevents them from seeing color). People affected by this disorder can only see black, white, and shades of gray.

**N**

**neutral**—the opposite of a hue. Black, white, and grays are considered neutrals and do not appear anywhere on the color wheel.

**O**

**opponent–process theory**—associated with the cones in the eye, it is the theory that when complementary colors are viewed, pairs of receptors cause one color to be inhibited when the other one is viewed.

**P**

**perception**—the ability to make sense of or understand visual stimuli.

**pigments**—the finely ground minerals, oxides, and chemicals that give paints, pastels, and other art media their color.

**pixel/pixelated**—the square two-dimensional picture elements of light that make up images in raster-based programs such as Photoshop.

**PostScript**—a page description language developed by Adobe, which tells the printer specifically how to create and print an image on a page.

**primary colors (hues)**—the three most basic hues—red, yellow, and blue—that make up all of the other colors.

**Q**

**quaternary colors**—hues that are made up of a tertiary and a primary or secondary color.

**R**

**radiance map**—a special algorithm that is used to predict the reaction of light falling on an object, creating the proper color relationship to the quality of light on a given surface. (*See also* **image-based lighting**.)

**raster-based programs**—software programs that render and work with pixels. An example of a raster-based program is Photoshop.

**raster image processor (RIP)**—works hand in hand with the PostScript language and interprets the data or code translating the instructions to the printer. A RIP is built into most desktop printers, but is a separate module for imagesetters.

**rasters**—rows of pixels.

**reflected beam**—the beam of light reflected off a given object that shows us its color.

**render/rendering**—the process by which the computer collects all of the data from the digital-animation program, the lighting, effects, and specified camera angles and compiles all of the information to videotape or film.

**resolution**—the number of pixels per inch making up a digital raster-based image.

**retinex theory**—theory developed by Edwin Land that states that no matter what the lighting conditions are, we expect an object to retain its color.

**rhodopsin**—the light-sensitive chemical agent in the rods in the eye. Also called *visual purple*.

**S**

**saturation**—the lightness or darkness of a hue. Also referred to as chroma, intensity, or brightness.

**secondary colors (hues)**—colors made by mixing equal parts of two primary hues together.

**sensation**—the response or reaction to a stimulus.

**separations**—plates made to be used in production printing, which correspond to the four colors (CMYK) of inks used in the printing process.

**shade**—a hue plus the addition of black.

**simultaneous contrast**—the effect of complementary colors to influence each other and the adjacent hues.

**site specific**—works of art that are developed for a specific location and may become part of that environment when finished.

**split complement**—a hue plus the two adjacent hues to its complement.

**successive contrast**—color phenomenon seen when the same hue is placed on differing background colors, that hue appears to change visually.

**synesthesia**—a form of color perception in which people perceive their environment by using a combination of two or more senses.

**T**

**tertiary colors**—colors made by combining a primary and a secondary color.

**tetrad**—four hues that are of equal distance from each other on the color wheel.

**texture map**—a skin that an animator applies over a wire frame, which consists of texture and color information.

**tiled/tiling**—also referred to as page tiling, an algorithm that is used to piece together a print from smaller segments.

**tint**—the hue plus the addition of white.

**tone**—the hue plus the addition of gray.

**triad**—three hues that are of equal distance from each other on the color wheel.

**trichromatic theory**—there are three types of cone pigment for sensing a different wavelength of light: blue-violet for short range, green for middle, and red for longest wavelengths.

**trompe l'oeil**—visual deception, from the French meaning "to fool the eye," in which objects are rendered in extremely fine detail.

**truth in materials**—Constantine Brancusi's philosophy that materials should not be painted or disguised, and that the natural beauty of the material should be displayed.

**twain acquire (TWAIN)**—the image-scanning software built into Adobe Photoshop. It stands for "technology without an interesting name."

## V

**value contrast**—the concept of how a color may appear when placed on a contrasting background.

**vector-based programs**—software programs that use a mathematical formula to create art or graphics. Examples of vector-based programs include Illustrator, FreeHand, and Flash.

**vehicle**—the agent used to suspend the pigment and aid in the flow of watercolors, oils, and acrylic paints.

## W

**wire frame**—a structure on which an animator can apply a skin that contains texture and color information called a texture map.

**wax bloom**—a white waxy build up that can occur in crayons and colored pencils. It happens when the wax base or binder of the medium begins to separate and bead up on the surface of a drawing.

**Index and Illustration List**

## Illustration List by Artist